The DEVIL'S TOWN

BOOKS BY PHILIP LEIGH

Southern Reconstruction

The Confederacy at Flood Tide:
The Political and Military Ascension, June to December 1862

Lee's Lost Dispatch and Other Civil War Controversies

Trading With the Enemy:
The Covert Economy During the American Civil War

Co. *Aytch* by Sam Watkins
Annotated and Illustrated by Philip Leigh

The Devil's Town
Hot Springs During the Gangster Era

PHILIIP LEIGH

SHOTWELL PUBLISHING
Columbia, South Carolina

THE DEVIL'S TOWN: HOT SPRINGS DURING THE GANGSTER ERA

Produced in the Republic of South Carolina by

Shotwell Publishing, LLC
Post Office Box 2592
Columbia, South Carolina 29202

www.ShotwellPublishing.com

Cover Images: New York Gangsters, World Telegram photo by Dick DeMarsico (Courtesy Library of Congress); Horses Racing at Oaklawn Park (Courtesy of Richard DeSpain)
Cover Design: Hazel's Dream / Boo Jackson TCB

ISBN-13: 978-1947660052
ISBN 10: 1947660055

10 9 8 7 6 5 4 3 2 1

The problem with fiction is that it has to be plausible. That's not true with non-fiction.

– Tom Wolfe

CONTENTS

Chapter One
INTRODUCTION

THE HISTORY OF HOT SPRINGS, Arkansas, during the gangster era is a story of a town at war with itself in a contest between illusion and reality.

Typical among the notorious visitors from the mid-1930s to mid-1950s was Meyer Lansky. He'd arrive with his oldest and crippled son, Buddy, who was born with spina bifida in 1930. Buddy took thermal baths at Levi Hospital in waters supplied by the forty-seven hot springs flowing from the lower slopes of 400-foot Hot Springs Mountain on the east side of the community's tiny downtown along Central Avenue. The springs released the water at a consistent 143° Fahrenheit, which a National Park Service reservoir cooled to 100° and piped to the bathhouses operating under strict government license. Although the hydrotherapy didn't cure Buddy, he welcomed it because he felt more nearly able-bodied when floating in pools of water. Meyer sometimes also took the spa, but he more often had fun in other ways. He liked horseback riding, golf and the readily available amusement of watching others gamble.

Except for a brief thoroughbred season at nearby Oaklawn Park, gambling was officially illegal in the town. In fact, it had been outlawed in the entire state since at least the adoption of the state's current constitution in 1874. Nonetheless, until 1967 illegal gambling often flourished in Hot Springs, which the religious elements in the state sometimes referred to as The Devil's Town. As late as 1964 a *New York Times* investigative journalist described it at the largest illegal gambling center in the country. To be sure, Las Vegas was bigger but gambling was legal in Nevada.

At times Hot Springs gambling was limited to private clubs whose members furtively included the guests of leading hotels, or covertly carried on in the backrooms of pool halls and tobacco shops. At other times it was brazen with neon lighted casinos and sidewalk loudspeakers announcing horse race results from all across America. Much depended upon a combination of who was mayor of the town and who was governor of the state.[1]

Neither Hot Springs nor Lansky let the law stand in the way of earning a living or having a good time. Games of chance had been popular in the town since at least the 1870s when Civil War veterans with persistent injuries travelled to the area for the palliative effects of the warm waters. Visitor growth accelerated after the federal government built a military hospital in 1887. Not until 1889 did a Norwegian immigrant living in Pittsburgh, Pennsylvania, invent an economical hot water storage tank. Prior to that, natural flowing hot springs were a rare luxury.[2]

The living standards of the residents gradually became dependent upon the earnings that gambling provided, which government authorities were bribed to ignore. By the 1930s eight illicit clubs functioned under the informal authority of gambling czar William Jacobs who operated the two largest ones, the Belvedere and the Southern Club. His insistence upon unrigged gaming put Hot Springs in good repute among America's high rollers, who sometimes referred to the town by the nickname, "Bubbles."[3]

Meyer Lansky | a Library of Congress

Shortly after arriving in New York in 1911 as a nine-year-old Jewish immigrant, Lansky quickly learned that he did not enjoy gambling. After realizing that he could not consistently win games of chance when he took to the streets to match pennies and shoot dice for nickels and dimes, the boy vowed he would not trust his future to luck. Instead he would make his own luck by arranging his affairs in a way that made winning inevitable, even at times when others assumed he was gambling.

Thereafter, he increasingly drifted toward a life of crime. By his mid-teens he was part of a gang headed by Charles "Lucky" Luciano, who had the common sense to admit talented non-Italians into his clique. How Charles gained the "Lucky" nickname is unclear, but it happened sometime while he was still in his twenties. It may have resulted from his habitual gambling, or it may have been a mispronunciation of his original Italian surname, Lucania. Finally, it could have stemmed from the fact that he unexpectedly survived several Mob-related assaults.

Shortly after the federal Volstead Act launched thirteen years of enforcement against the recreational use of alcoholic beverages in 1920, Lansky joined with fellow Jewish gangster Benjamin "Bugsy"

Siegel to form the Bug and Meyer Mob. At the tender ages of fifteen and nineteen respectively, the two became hired killers for various New York and New Jersey bootlegging gangs.[4]

The older and smarter Lansky assumed leadership. As the duo gradually hired other executioners they gathered a reputation for dependability and skill in their nefarious work. Their rates, however, grew increasingly expensive until they were cut-in as junior partners with some of the biggest bootleggers in the New York area where Luciano had meanwhile climbed into the upper echelon of the Sicilian Mafia.

When the two top 1920s Sicilian bosses went to war against each other, the younger Luciano foresaw that he must overthrow both of them. Their belligerent personalities and refusals to cooperate with non-Sicilian mobsters were likely to lead to endless inter-Mob warfare and deny all gangs the shared benefits of cooperation. His ally Lansky, for example, appreciated that coordinated methods of bribing the police could benefit all Mob groups.

Luciano and Lansky also anticipated opportunities in other types of rackets whereas the existing Sicilian bosses were chiefly interested in continuing to dominate the bootlegging business. The prejudice of the incumbent leaders against inter-Mob cooperation caused steady losses to all the gangs as each band occasionally hijacked the beer and liquor shipments of the others in a zero-sum attempt to acquire free—meaning stolen—inventory.[5]

In 1931 Luciano hired Bugsy Siegel, who recruited three other gunmen, and executed one of the older Sicilian bosses. The other incumbent immediately sensed Lucky's ambition to assume overall command and engaged another gunman to pre-emptively murder both Luciano and Lansky. Moments before the killer was to pull the trigger, however, four of Lansky's gunmen murdered the assassin's client thereby leaving the killer with no reason to execute Luciano and Lansky.[6]

Lucky became the new boss in the early 1930s and transformed the two previously rival organizations into the American Mafia. Although Sicilians would dominate the resultant structure, cooperation with non-Italian gangs was no longer forbidden. In 1931 Lucky invited the major Mafia families to a Chicago assembly in order to organize an oversight commission, which was to function like a mobsters' version of the Supreme Court. Each family became a commission member, entitled to a single vote. Territorial and other disputes were to be settled by majority votes. The five New York families had the biggest influence because no other city had more than a single family represented on the commission.

Luciano was too shrewd to appoint himself as boss-of-bosses. He wanted to avoid making himself vulnerable to the type of revolt and assassination plot that he had led against the older predecessors. Instead he became a *quasi* administrator for the commission, which operated like a rule-making cabinet as well as a Supreme Court. Other Mafia members, however, generally realized that Luciano was basically the "greatest among equals."[7]

Mafia membership required a lifelong commitment and a code of silence toward outsiders. Although cooperation with Jewish, Irish, and other gangs had become permissible, only men with two Italian parents were formally accepted into the families. Anticipating the repeal of Prohibition in 1933, the national Mafia syndicate took control of prostitution, narcotics, gambling, loan-sharking and the labor rackets. Only marginally profitably activities were leftover for independent outlaws.[8]

In fairness to Italian-Americans, however, two points should be clarified. First, based merely on census data less than one-tenth of one percent of the ethnic group was connected with the Mafia. Second, Italian immigrants were sometimes unfairly stereotyped as Mafia partly because they first settled in the crime-prone big city ghettos.

But crime was only one method of escaping the ghettos. Professional sport was another. Consider, for example, the evolution of the leading cultural groups at the top of professional boxing. Early in the twentieth century they were mostly Irish. Shortly thereafter Jews replaced them and next the Italians. By the 1960s most winning boxers were blacks or Latinos. As other paths opened and families moved out of the ghettos, athletic young Irishmen, Jews, Italians, blacks, and Latinos sequentially left boxing. Presently, for example, heavyweight boxing is far less popular than when the various ethnic groups noted above were contending for leadership in America's ghettos.

The evolution of the chief ethnic outlaw groups was similar. Italian Americans acquired a gangster reputation partly because they were attempting to escape the ghettos at the dawn of Prohibition. Bootlegging profits were so large and easily earned that the memory of such illegal prosperity tempted Mafia veterans for decades after the end of Prohibition to try to replicate the easy success with other illegal schemes. As the generation gradually died out, however, other ethnicities became increasingly identified as the stereotypical American gangster.[9]

At the urging of Luciano-Lansky allies like Frank Costello, the Mafia families began systematically bribing government authorities to protect Mob interests in the early 1930s. Costello gained control of ten out of sixteen district leaders of New York City's Tammany Hall Democratic political machine. Luciano and Costello even accompanied the Tammany delegation to the 1932 Democratic presidential convention. While Luciano initially put his support behind former New York governor Al Smith who had been the 1928 presidential nominee, Costello later convinced him to back the eventual winner, Franklin D. Roosevelt.[10]

Luciano's American Mafia also formed a new internal enforcement agency as a successor to the Bug and Meyer Mob. The new centralized agency, known as Murder Inc., could send executioners anywhere. They had less chance of getting caught than local operatives because the local police had difficulty identifying a motive when killers swooped in from out of town and quickly vanished afterward.

Mob kingpins insisted that Murder Inc.'s services could only be engaged by partners in the American Mafia and even then only for purposes of executing condemned members. Contracts against outsiders were forbidden. As shall be explained in chapter three, the infamous Dutch Schultz would be executed specifically because he intended to disobey the rule. Costello emphasized that murdering non-gangsters would undermine the police and the corrupted government protection that he had worked so painstakingly to secure. Murder, Inc. slayings required a unanimous vote of the top leaders such as Luciano, Lansky, and Costello. Jews were often deliberately selected as the contract killers in order to insulate Italian mobsters from direct culpability.[11]

Murder, Inc. killed a hundred or more victims before the organization unraveled in the 1940s when one member turned state's evidence. The "canary" told Brooklyn district attorney William O'Dwyer that he could provide details on eighty-five murders. Eventually eight mobsters went to the electric chair and fifty to prison. While interrogations were still in progress, however, the snitch "went out the window" from an upper floor of a New York hotel room despite a heavy guard. Lansky later said that Costello paid a $100,000 bribe to demonstrate that "the canary who could sing couldn't fly."[12]

The police guards were never convicted of a crime, partly because O'Dwyer testified on their behalf. But they were demoted from plainclothesmen to uniformed cops. Although O'Dwyer said that his prosecution against the most notorious Murder, Inc. suspects went out the window with "the canary," he gained enough favorable publicity to be elected New York City mayor in 1945.

Four years later, however, he denounced an investigation into Brooklyn police corruption by the borough's new district attorney who was a political enemy. After nineteen police were indicted O'Dwyer resigned as mayor. President Truman gave him a face-saving appointment as Ambassador to Mexico where O'Dwyer said he was going to "fight communism."[13]

Although Hot Springs had long been a wide-open town it became an increasingly attractive haven to big-time mobsters like those mentioned above after Owney Madden moved there in 1934. The forty-three year old Madden had first built a gangster reputation in New York. After his father died, the boy immigrated to New York from Liverpool, England, in 1903. Upon arriving in Manhattan at age twelve he lived with his mom and siblings in the Hell's Kitchen neighborhood along the west side of mid-town. He soon joined a local gang, became an expert mugger and was earning $200 a day before he was out of his teens.

Owney Madden | Courtesy of Garland County Historical Society

Hollywood star George Raft was one of his childhood buddies and based his gangster film portrayals on Madden's mannerisms. Owney likely committed his first murder at age seventeen and killed four more men by the time he was twenty-three. He was prompted to make one killing in 1910 merely because the victim had tried to date one of Madden's girlfriends. Although the slaying took place aboard a public trolley among many witnesses, police could not persuade anyone to testify afterward, despite catching Owney in a daring rooftop chase.[14]

When he reached age twenty in 1912 a rival gang tried to kill him. Despite absorbing eleven bullets he survived. He refused, however, to identify his attackers to the police. "It's nobody's business but mine," he said. Instead his own gang retaliated and killed six of the assailants before Owney was even released from the hospital.

During his outpatient convalescence, however, a competitor within his own gang tried to assume control by arguing that Owney was permanently crippled and therefore unsuited for leadership. Although Owney later arranged for hired killers to murder his rival, three witnesses who knew of the pact violated their oaths of silence. As a result Owney was convicted of manslaughter and given a ten-to-twenty year prison sentence. He remained in New York's Sing-Sing prison for about a decade until released on probation in 1923 when he was thirty-one years old.[15]

At the height of Prohibition he formed a new gang and went into bootlegging. Prohibition revolutionized crime because it was exceptionally profitable. Future Mafia boss Joseph Bonanno, who immigrated into America during the era, marveled, "When I first got into bootlegging, I thought it was too good to be true. I didn't consider it wrong. It seemed fairly safe and the police didn't bother you."[16]

For large sectors of the public, violating the Volstead Act evolved into a type of sport. New York Governor Al Smith served liquor at public receptions. New York City Mayor Jimmy Walker seldom arrived in his office before noon because he spent most nights carousing at speakeasies. Since the national law was unpopular, some states adopted weak regulations that permitted their state police to avoid enforcing the federal law. New York state was among them.

Consequently, enforcement fell to the Treasury Department's Prohibition Bureau. But it became a laughing stock because politically appointed flunkies, incompetents and corrupt administrators staffed it. Owney thrived in such an environment. Among his partners was Joseph P. Kennedy, the father of future President John Kennedy. In order to maximize profits, Owney produced his own beer brand, *Madden's Number One.* It cost about $5 dollars a barrel to make but sold to speakeasies for $36.[17]

Madden also operated a outwardly legitimate coal delivery and laundering businesses as well as Harlem's famous Cotton Club where jazz greats like Duke Ellington performed and Lena Horne joined the chorus line at age 16. Despite being English, Owney moved as an equal in Mafia circles that included Italians and Jews such as Luciano, Lansky, Siegel, and Costello. When one young trigger-happy hoodlum tried to muscle in on his rum-running business in 1932, Owney occupied him on a telephone conversation while the interloper was in a phone a booth. During the lengthy talk, Owney had the booth's location call-traced and sent hired killers to gun down his enemy.[18]

The murder happened at a bad time for Owney because his probation board had been accumulating evidence that he was not giving up his wicked ways. The board threatened deportation or re-imprisonment. Simultaneously, Prohibition was ending and the Italians were taking control of the remaining rackets. Since the easy pickings of the Prohibition Era in New York were over, Madden was casting about for new business lines that would not conflict with the plans of the Italians who dominated the Mafia at the time.

Professional boxing promotion was an early example of his diversifying efforts where he gained early success. In one case he backed the giant six-foot-seven-inch Primo Carnera who won the 1933 World Heavyweight Championship title. But Carnera was overrated and Owney may have helped him win his title by reason of a series of fixed fights in which some of the losers were paid to let him win. Nonetheless, Owney also had relationships with other famous fighters such as Max Baer and Rocky Marciano who became lifelong friends.[19]

About a year before his probation board began questioning Owney about suspected parole violations, he took his first trip to Hot Springs in 1932. At the time, Las Vegas and Miami were practically wastelands. In contrast, Hot Springs was a wide-open town with a reputation for welcoming visiting mobsters as long as they behaved peacefully. Since Madden also still carried five of the eleven bullets he took in 1912, he may have also sought relief in the thermal waters. Contemporary mobster Dutch Schultz recommended that he visit the spa and make a point of meeting the young lady who worked at a gift shop near the town's prime hotel, the Arlington.

Madden pulled up in an impressive Duesenberg and parked in front of thirty-year-old Agnes Demby's shop. From Agnes's viewpoint behind the counter the grand convertible filled both picture windows. After the well-dressed driver entered the shop, Agnes told another clerk that she would attend to the new customer. Owney looked around and talked with her as he gradually bought an increasing number of items. By the time he was finished he had spent about a thousand dollars, which was a huge amount in the depths of the Great Depression. Thus, he felt justified in asking

Agnes on a dinner date. But she modestly turned him down and went home where she lived with her widowed dad who was the town's postmaster.

Since her father was not at home when Agnes arrived, she grew bored and walked over to the Arlington lobby where she found Owney sitting and talking with another guy. She walked up to the pair and asked Owney if he'd still like to have dinner. The generous mobster gave her a broad smile and said that he'd love to.

Madden stayed for two more weeks and spent most of his time with Agnes. The more familiar he became with Agnes and Hot Springs the more he envisioned a promising future for the two of them as well as the town. Agnes would become the love of his life and Hot Springs held potential to become his miniature New York with no rival big-time gangsters in permanent residence.[20]

Later that year Agnes visited him in New York and Owney reciprocated by returning afterward for a second Hot Springs visit. But the parole board continued to bedevil him. Evidently, somebody—he never learned whom—wanted him returned to Sing Sing. During one hearing an inspector informed the board that Madden had been arrested 140 times but only convicted once, which was the 1912 manslaughter case. FBI director J. Edgar Hoover jumped on the bandwagon merely because he was annoyed after a newspaper had photographed Madden while his own agents had never been able to do so, despite Hoover's orders.[21]

In a bid to project a hard-on-crime image New York Governor and presidential hopeful, Franklin Roosevelt, put his weight behind the parole board. An investigative committee of the legislature had discovered problems not only with Madden, but also with other notables, including New York City Mayor Jimmy Walker. Only days before the Democratic presidential nominating convention, however, Roosevelt passed the basket of hot potatoes to the conflicted Mayor Walker.

Gangsters Lansky and, as noted, Luciano and Costello attended the convention as power brokers for the Tammany machine. According to Madden biographer Graham Nown, the likely candidates could not gain the Democratic Party nomination without assuring Mayor Walker and his pals, including Owney, that the legal pressures against them would be lifted. When Luciano told Al Smith that Tammany had decided to back Roosevelt, Smith replied, "Charlie, Frank Roosevelt will break his word to you."[22]

Frank Costello | Library of Congress

Smith was right. Once Roosevelt got the nomination Walker was forced to resign and everything fell apart for Owney. The parole board used a technicality to order him back to jail. His chauffer drove him to Sing Sing where a guard doubted the unescorted Owney's identity and initially refused to admit him. But by sundown July 7, 1932, Madden was back in a prison cell. In November the board ruled that he must serve twelve months, which meant that he would have to wait a year before he could restart life with Agnes.[23]

Since Prohibition had been abolished before he was released in July 1933 Madden turned his attention to the gambling rackets. Gambling casinos were illegal nearly everywhere in America but—as they did for the Prohibition Era speakeasies—authorities often winked at them. When stating his opinion about the desirability of peaceably dividing the illegal gambling territories among the various Mafia families instead of fighting over them, the influential Lansky told other Mafia leaders that the country was big enough for everyone to have a piece of the action without fighting one another.

But Lansky preferred that casino owners be men he knew personally. Except for his uncertain parole status, it looked like Owney could turn Hot Springs into his little corner of the game. Unfortunately, his parole required that he not leave New York State. Nonetheless, through mysterious negotiations his parole was eventually transferred to Hot Springs, conditional to his remaining in Arkansas. Thus, he could not easily continue as a boxing promoter.[24]

Outsiders have never known why the New York parole board reversed its attitude toward Madden. Even after he was released from prison in 1933, investigations revealed probable corruption in his outwardly legitimate coal supply business. Board members may have been bribed, or they might just simply have decided that Madden was small potatoes after the end of Prohibition. According to biographer Nown, boss Frank Costello's everybody-gets-his-share leadership principle probably played a role. [25]

One of Owney's future Hot Springs confidants, attorney Q. Byrum Hurst, said that the process involved many months of negotiation and included participants who were among America's most prominent leaders. Nobody else has ever explained much about how Owney's probation troubles ended. One parole commissioner, however, indicated that he approved Owney's transfer to Hot Springs partly because the gangster was ill. He also half-humorously suggested that he was happy to get Owney out of town so that the police would not need to hunt him down if there were new unexplained gangster murders in New York. [26]

During the summer of 1934 Mob leaders met privately at New York's Waldorf Astoria hotel to divide up the rackets controlled by Dutch Schultz who, they assumed, would soon be headed to jail for income tax evasion. During the meeting, Lansky awarded Owney Miami's Tropical Park horse race track and told him that he could also be the Mob's representative in Hot Springs.

Owney married Agnes in November 1935 at a private ceremony in nearby Sheridan, Arkansas. The wedding site resulted from Agnes's vanity. If they had been married in Garland County, where Hot Springs was the county seat, the local newspapers would have reported the ages of the husband and wife as shown on the marriage certificate. Agnes was a few years older than she publicly admitted. The couple would live in Hot Springs for the rest of their lives. The marriage ended at Owney's death in 1965. Agnes never remarried and lived until 1991 when she died at age 90.[27]

---

1 Wallace Turner, "Hot Springs: Gamblers' Haven," *New York Times*, March 8, 1964, available https://goo.gl/dcrZzh [Accessed July 7, 2017]; Robert Boyle, "The Hottest Spring in Hot Springs," Sports Illustrated, March 19, 1962, available http://on.si.com/2tzoHI8 [Accessed: July 7, 2017]

2 Francis Scully, *Hot Springs Arkansas and Hot Spring National Park* (Little Rock, Ark.: Pioneer Press, 1966), 157; Dee Brown, *The American Spa: Hot Springs, Arkansas* (Little Rock, Ark.: Rose Publishing, 1982), 40, 50; Mary Bellis, "History of the Water Heater—Invented by Henry Ruud," *ThoughtCo*, August 23, 2016, available https://goo.gl/dcrZzh [Accessed: July 7, 2017]

3 Orval Allbritton, *The Mob at The Spa* (Hot Springs, Ark.: Garland County Historical Society, 2011), 168-169, 172

4 Carl Sifakis, *The Mafia Encyclopedia*: 3rd Edition (New York: Checkmark Books, 2005), 68; Selwyn Rabb, *Five Families: The Rise, Decline and Resurgence of America's Most Powerful Mafia Empires* (New York: St. Martin's Press, 2006), 30

5 Selwyn Rabb, *Five Families*, 28

6 Carl Sifakis, *The Mafia Encyclopedia*: 3rd Edition, 280

7 Selwyn Rabb, *Five Families*, 33-34

8 *Ibid.*, 50

9 Richard Sasuly, *Bookies and Bettors* (New York: Holt, Reinhart, and Winston, 1982), 141-42

10 Thomas Reppetto, *American Mafia: A History of its Rise to Power* (New York: Henry Holt & Co., 2004), 146; Arkansas Senator Joseph T. Robinson was Smith's Vice-Presidential running mate in 1928 when Robinson was also the Senate Minority Leader.

11 Selwyn Rabb, *Five Families*, 67

12 Carl Sifakis, *The Mafia Encyclopedia*: 3rd Edition, 321; Selwyn Rabb, Five Families, 69

13 Thomas Reppetto, *American Mafia*, 224-25, 231-32

14 Orval Allbritton, *The Mob at the Spa*, 212; Carl Sifakis, *The Mafia Encyclopedia*: 3rd Edition, 285-86; Graham Nown, *Arkansas Godfather* (Little Rock, Ark.: Butler Center Books, 2011), 17

15 Graham Nown, *Arkansas Godfather*, 68-9

16 Selwyn Rabb, *Five Families*, 24

17 *Ibid.*, 24-25; Graham Nown, *Arkansas Godfather*, 11; Thomas Reppetto, *American Mafia*, 109

18 Carl Sifakis, *The Mafia Encyclopedia*: 3rd Edition, 106; Graham Nown, *Arkansas Godfather*, 11, 221

19 Graham Nown, *Arkansas Godfather*, 156-57, 221, 320

20 *Ibid.*, 198-204

21 *Ibid.*, 223, 227

22 *Ibid.*, 236-41

23 *Ibid.*, 244-45, 51

24 *Ibid.*, 266

25 *Ibid.*, 278

26 *Ibid.*, 266-69

27 *Ibid.*, 275, 280; Orval Allbritton, *The Mob at the Spa*, 213

Chapter Two
ASSIMILATION

WHEN ILLEGAL GAMBLING THRIVED in Hot Springs, prosecution largely defaulted to local authorities due to the historically weak status of Arkansas governors. Disgusted with the corruption of the carpetbag era, Arkansas voters thereafter limited the powers of the state's central government in favor of localism. Consequently, the state's 1874 constitution restricted the governor's term to two years and permitted the legislature to convene only once every other year.

Since the state was also persistently one of the nation's poorest, her governors constantly had more pressing problems than illegal gambling, especially because it was mostly isolated in a single one of Arkansas's seventy-five counties. The combination of gambling's extraordinary profitability and the embarrassingly low salaries of Arkansas's executive officers perpetuated a temptation for bribery. Hot Springs's gaming interests readily perceived that consistent pay-offs to state government officials might persuade them to leave the enforcement of Arkansas's anti-gambling laws in the hands of local authorities. Given the combination of circumstances, it is hard to avoid concluding that at least some governors yielded to the temptation.[28]

As late as the 1950s and 60s when Orval Faubus was governor, FBI agent Clay White concluded that such payments were made two ways. First were the election year contributions, which typically totaled $50,000 to $75,000. Second were regular monthly payments that totaled about $75,000 annually. Although Faubus claimed he never received any of it, his biographer, Roy Reed, wrote, "The money was picked up [in Hot Springs] every Saturday night by a high state official, stowed in a black bag and delivered to Little Rock," which is the capital city.[29]

Similarly, a sister of Hot Springs Municipal Judge Verne Ledgerwood who operated the local political machine in tandem with Mayor Leo McLaughlin from 1927 to 1947 later averred that her brother and the mayor were briefed by at least one governor's aide to deliver any "gift" to a small storage closet near the governor's office at the state capitol. She said that Hot Springs officials complied several times but never saw who picked-up the envelopes they put in the closet. A venerable reporter for one of the local newspapers also later claimed that a standard annual contribution to a cooperating governor during that period was $50,000.[30]

When Owney permanently joined Agnes in Hot Springs, the rowdy town's power structure was much like New York's, only in miniature. The casinos, bookies, brothels and nightclubs bribed local law enforcement in order to insure that raids against violators were only erratic and generally signaled secretly in advance. While the resulting fines were small enough to be absorbed as a routine business expense, publicity about the raids was prominent and enabled the legal authorities to create the illusion of enforcement. Mayor McLaughlin and Judge Ledgerwood were the power brokers when Owney moved to town.

Soon after arriving, Owney met the two leaders. They explained that he was welcome as a resident so long as he remained on good behavior. Initially he was informally forbidden to buy an interest in any local gambling operations. McLaughlin and Ledgerwood feared that mere rumors suggesting that a recently paroled New York gangster was moving into the town's gaming business might trigger incremental pressure from state authorities to close everything down. After he was quietly absorbed into the community over a number of years, however, the pair hinted that Madden might then be permitted to become a part owner of some of the clubs.[31]

Mayor McLaughlin was a hinterland version of New York City Mayor Jimmy Walker. The Manhattan playboy even became friendly with his remote double and visited McLaughlin in Hot Springs where they were photographed at least once sharing Leo's booth at Oaklawn Park horse track. Like Walker, Leo was often in the company of attractive young ladies.[32]

Pulled by two horses named Scotch and Soda during good weather, Leo took daily carriage rides thorough the downtown area while dressed in a riding outfit that included a signature fresh carnation in his lapel. He did not marry until he was thirty years old and ended his third marriage when he was forty-eight in 1936. Over the next nine years he was a bachelor mayor.

He was a fiery campaigner. Political speeches often morphed into theatrical performances, as Leo progressively removed his coat and rolled up his sleeves to continue the monologues. His political machine was so powerful that only a single opponent challenged him at the polls during his twenty-year rule.[33]

In addition to the ordinary device of political patronage available to politicians in New York and elsewhere, Mayor McLaughlin utilized an extra tool that made his machine almost invincible. Specifically, Arkansas's poll tax could be illegally manipulated to create fraudulent votes. The state's poll tax dated from the antebellum era and originally was unrelated to voting rights. It started as merely a per capita tax on all adult male citizens. By the end of the nineteenth century, however, anyone wishing to vote was required to show a receipt for his poll tax. When Arkansas women were later included in the electorate they too were required to present poll tax receipts before voting. The one-dollar tax was used to pay for public schools.

Arkansas was a rural state where many farmers only infrequently visited the county seats or other towns where sheriffs had offices to accept poll tax payments and issue receipts. Consequently, a state law had long permitted a citizen to instruct a substitute to pay his tax for him. The statute envisioned that farmers running errands in a receipt-issuing town might pay the poll tax for a small number of other family members with the probable understanding that each voter would reimburse him when he returned home. No personal identification was required to pay the tax and collect the receipt.[34]

Although a 1935 state law prohibited the wholesale purchase of receipts for non-family members, the statute was widely ignored. The commendable public-school-funding purpose of the tax was a convenient rationalization for disregarding the law. Consequently, key supporters of the McLaughlin Machine would each "purchase" hundreds, or more, poll tax receipts that would be handed out to vagrants and prostitutes on Election Day in any race where a

Machine candidate was challenged. Often a two-dollar bill was pinned to each receipt. Election officials also frequently ignored the requirement that the receipts be initialed or stamped at the polling places and thereby cancelled in the way of a used postage stamp. As a result, some were undoubtedly used multiple times by people who fraudulently voted at more than one precinct.[35]

The total number of receipt-manipulated votes stolen by McLaughlin's apparatus in any given election will never be known. However, as shall be explained in a chapter eight, near the end of his term a young group of World War II veterans successfully challenged his organization by exposing poll tax fraud.[36]

An earlier criminal case involving McLaughlin's younger brother George demonstrated that the mayor's corruption was not limited to white-collar crimes such as poll tax fraud. In 1933, two years before Owney Madden settled in the town, a small-time hotel operator used George as a silent partner to win political approval to operate a number of slot machines around town at cigar stores, pool halls and other back street dives. In order to avoid conflict with the "respectable" casinos and nightclubs, George's one-arm bandits were nickel and quarter units. One winter night George got a phone call from his operating partner.

The colleague explained that an off-duty taxi driver named Sidney Long hit the jackpot on one of the nickel machines and walked off with $18. The complaint was not that Long had won, but that he had been using slugs instead of coins. George rushed over to his partner's office to get the details and ended up phoning the Yellow Cab office looking for Long who was out driving his cab at the time. George told the taxi night supervisor where George would be waiting and asked the supervisor to tell Long that George wanted to see him when Long returned to the taxi office.

When he finally got George's message Long met him at the slot machine partner's office where a physical fight began almost immediately. Long escaped to return to the Yellow Cab office closely pursued by George, his partner, and another ruffian. Witnesses stated that McLaughlin next pulled a colt revolver and smashed Long over the head with its barrel. He then hit the victim several times with a blackjack and searched Long's pockets evidently looking for the ill-gotten slot machine winnings. Afterwards Long went to the Army-Navy Hospital for treatment. He was released, but two days later visited a second doctor who recommended that he return to the hospital again. Five days after his beating Long died at the hospital where his death was officially attributed to head injuries.[37]

Long's demise was too widely known to prevent newspaper inquiries, but reporters were soon complaining that the Hot Springs police were saying little. One newspaper finally suggested that the silence signified a cover-up. Although Leo did not want his brother indicted, the prosecuting attorney and the local state circuit court judge, Earl Witt, said that the publicity made it impossible to avoid an indictment.

Witt helped devise a pro-McLaughlin reaction plan. George and his two accomplices were to be arrested, but released on $3,000 bail each. A subsequent grand jury, whose foreman was a McLaughlin Machine relative (Cecil Ledgerwood), dropped the charges against the two accessories. Although George was charged with murder he was represented by two accomplished criminal lawyers and pled self-defense.

George's version of events conceded that he battered Long, but only after the latter attacked him. He explained that he politely approached Long to ask that Long pay for a check written by Long's girlfriend that had bounced. According to George, Long flew into a rage and started the fight. George admitted hitting Long with both the barrel of his pistol and a black jack, but only to counter the attack.

After the initial clash, George said he was contrite and decided to follow Long to the taxicab office where he hoped that their differences might be settled peaceably. Instead, George claimed, Long viciously attacked him a second time. When asked of reports that he was angry about Long's use of slot machine slugs, George replied that the slug allegation was not pertinent to him because he was merely a police clerk and had no other job. He claimed he was neither an operator nor part owner of slot machines.

The story was incredible and could only be told without being laughed out of court because six prosecution witnesses were missing. All promptly left town before the ink was dry on their subpoenas. Among them was Long's girlfriend who allegedly wrote the bad check. Somehow the witnesses unexpectedly came into money that enabled them to leave town for vacations and other visits.

When questioned about carrying a pistol, George explained that his police clerk job gave him the right to do so. But he was forced to admit that despite his authority he never made an arrest and that the bad check written by Long's girlfriend is the only one he ever tried to collect. The mayor also helped George by claiming, without support, that the hospital doctors were responsible for Long's death.

Jury tampering was also suspected. Five days after the trial ended one juror, a widow, was pleased to learn that her son had been hired as a fireman on the mayor's recommendation. Prior to Long's death she had repeatedly tried without success to get the young man a municipal job.

Additionally, the prosecutor had exhausted all of his challenges before the last jury member was selected. When Judge Witt instructed the sheriff to bring in a reserve juror, the last member turned out to be an alderman with close ties to the mayor. Judge Witt overruled the prosecutor's objection to admitting the alderman into the jury because Witt ruled that the DA had exhausted his allowed number of uncontestable challenges. The jury deliberated for less than an hour before returning George's not guilty verdict. Despite vanishing shortly after Long's death, the slot machines were back in operation soon after the trial ended.[38]

Although Leo was not as prone to violence as George, he had a broadminded attitude toward the law when a relaxation of its restraints might benefit the local economy or his personal interests. For about a dozen years before he was first elected mayor at age thirty-nine in 1927, Hot Springs had been ruled by reform mayors who forced gambling to go underground much like the speakeasies of the 1920s.

Part of Leo's winning campaign strategy was to indirectly promise a wider tolerance for gambling and similar entertainment.

While he never explicitly said he would permit showy casinos to reopen, his political speeches suggested that the town's quiet nightlife signified that business conditions could be improved if more amusements were readily available. When telling a group of voters that he had recently walked along Central Avenue around eight o'clock at night and noticed the street to be so deserted that he could have emptied a repeating rifle magazine down it without hitting anyone. He emphasized that the town's spa economy would descend into unimportance if it did not provide more libertine entertainment to attract well-heeled visitors.

Arkansas political history expert and Faubus biographer Roy Reed explained that Leo promised voters he would finance municipal improvements by regularly fining gamblers, bars, and prostitutes as an *ad hoc* form of substitute taxation. But the fines would be assessed in a manner that would enable the paymasters to continue their illegal operations, thereby providing a steady stream of cash flow into the city treasury. Among the improvements promised were new streets and sewers as well as a new fire station.

Jimmy Walker & Leo McLaughlin | Courtesy of Mary Hudgins Collection, University of Arkansas Libraries

The campaign was difficult, especially since Leo was running as a candidate without party affiliation in a general election during an era when nearly all Arkansas elections were settled in the Democratic primaries. As in many Southern states at the time, Arkansas general elections were usually mere formalities in which the Democratic primary winners trounced token opposition. When Richard Nixon carried the state in 1972 he was the first GOP presidential candidate to do so in a century. Nonetheless, McLaughlin won by 122 votes when the last reporting boxes, from his home ward, were counted.[39]

The power behind the throne, however, was Municipal Court Judge Verne Ledgerwood. His was a part-time job that normally required the judge to rule on minor violations, such as disturbing the peace. The rest of his time was devoted to private law practice. In 1927, however, Arkansas had no state police. Thus, even though gambling was illegal throughout the state, the various county sheriffs and municipal police departments normally enforced state laws as well as those applicable to their specific localities. Arkansas did not form a state police unit until 1935. Moreover, for many years thereafter it functioned mostly as an umbrella organization for various public safety departments such as the highway patrol.

Because the Hot Springs police department enforced his rulings, Judge Ledgerwood wanted a police chief who would reliably apply his verdicts. Since he was not satisfied with the chief who held office when the election approached, he asked the Democratic mayoral nominee if he would replace the man. After the nominee told the judge that he would not, Ledgerwood encouraged McLaughlin run for mayor as an independent. The judge promised Leo that he would support him on the condition that Leo appoint Verne's brother-in-law, Joe Wakelin, as police chief, assuming that Leo would be elected.

Leo made the appointment after he won the election and granted the judge a bonus by also choosing Verne's law partner, Allan T. "Sonny" Davies, as city attorney. It was the very post that Leo was leaving to become mayor. As a legislator ten years earlier, Davies successfully sponsored a bill—perhaps at Ledgerwood's urging—that authorized Hot Springs to create a municipal court. Whatever Davies's motivation, Ledgerwood won the first election to be the court's judge and had held the post ever since.[40]

As shall be explained, Wakelin would later be investigated for a variety of crimes and eventually sentenced to a two-year prison term. Unlike Wakelin, Davies was more widely known and admired. He was a World War I veteran, esteemed especially for having been admitted into the selective Army Air Corps, the forerunner of today's Air Force. But after later becoming a part of McLaughlin's Machine, Davies helped Mafia kingpin Lucky Luciano fight extradition to New York as shall be explained in the next chapter. Davies would also later represent McLaughlin's Machine against challenges of voter fraud.

Like the mayor, Judge Legderwood had a brother with suspicious connections to a murder although the brother was neither convicted nor even charged. On the advice of a doctor, Verne's tubercular older brother, Archie, moved to El Paso, Texas in 1922 in order to benefit from its dry climate. After his condition improved he returned to Hot Springs in 1931 when Verne helped him get a job at the Club Belvedere, which was a luxury casino a little north of town. Partly because he was satisfied with Archie's work and partly to ingratiate himself with the judge, about five years later the Belvedere owner—Bill Jacobs— offered to sell Archie a combined one-quarter interest in the Belvedere together with the Southern Club, which was one of the leading downtown casinos.

Although offered a bargain price of $15,000, Archie did not have the money. Consequently, Jacobs introduced him to an out of town acquaintance, Ed Ballard, who loaned Archie the funds at usurious rates. When the note came due in October 1936, Ballard returned to Hot Springs to collect. Archie would later claim that he paid Ballard $20,500 in cash.

Neither Ballard, who was found dead of gunshot wounds in his hotel room two days later, nor any third party ever confirmed that Ballard had received the money. Along with Ballard, an acquaintance, Robert Alexander, was also found in the room. Alexander, however, was alive but badly injured with two gunshot wounds. He did not live long enough to explain what had happened. The guest in an adjacent room was a vacationing Chicago Cubs radio announcer who was in his room at the time of the shooting. He told investigators that he did not hear any sounds of argument or struggle from Ballard's room prior the shots, one of which penetrated the wall into broadcaster's room.

Ultimately Hot Springs detectives decided that one of the men killed the other and then committed suicide. The incident resulted, they reasoned, from business disagreements between Ballard and Alexander. The chief detective told the press that Ballard had once filed a $250,000 breach of contract lawsuit against Alexander. The county coroner supported the detective's murder-suicide assumption and concluded that no inquest was required. Nonetheless, authorities never learned what became of the $20,500

Archie supposedly gave to Ballard. It was neither in the room nor the hotel's lobby safe.[41]

Gambling czar William S. Jacobs was the third pillar in the Hot Springs power structure when Madden arrived. Jacobs kept gaming on the level so that loaded dice, tilted tables, rigged slot machines and other swindles did not cheat the public. As noted, valid gaming tables, card-decks and dice encouraged visits from out of town big spenders thereby benefiting the entire community. In order to block out of town and gangster control, Jacobs required that local citizens be the primary owners of the town's clubs, casinos, slot joints, and bookmakers.

He also controlled local competition by requiring that new entrants gain his approval before entering the market. Although his blessings were not official requirements, any facility entering the business without them might encounter a multitude of harassments ranging from building code violations to unexplained outbreaks of fire on their premises. Jacobs also wanted to limit the number of operators in order to avoid the scrutiny that unrestricted growth might otherwise attract from the state capitol at Little Rock.

Not the least of Jacobs's accomplishments was a method for each illegal operator to compensate government officials in exchange for tolerating gambling while simultaneously creating the illusion that the laws against it were enforced. Hot Springs ordinances classified the operation of a gambling facility as a misdemeanor, which was legally no more serious than commercial violations of blue laws that required most businesses to be closed on Sunday. Businesses that violated the gambling and blue laws were each subject to fines ranging from $10 to $25. In order to avoid penalizing the patrons,

Jacobs required that each gaming operator charged with a violation appear in Ledgerwood's municipal court to pay the applicable fine. If they did not pay, they were shut down.

Finally, Jacobs arranged that an envelope of money was available for Elmer Walters to deliver to the mayor's office every Monday. The cash represented contributions from all the operators generally based upon their business volume. Although Elmer was listed on the Hot Springs fire department payroll, he had no official duties with the department.

Jacobs was fifty-one years old when McLaughlin was elected mayor in 1927. He grew up in Tennessee and lost a leg as a youth when working for a railroad in the middle part of the state. Thereafter he moved to Memphis where he learned the payoff techniques of running a successful illegal gambling club, which he sold in 1907 at age thirty. Flush with cash he moved to Hot Springs where he initially opened a movie theater during the silent film era. Within a few years he returned to illegal gaming and became partners with the local owners of the Southern and Ohio Clubs. Both were well-established casinos in the tiny Hot Springs downtown district along Central Avenue.

By 1913, however, the town had been overrun by rigged gaming operators and medical quacks falsely promising miracle hydrotherapy cures from the natural hot spring waters. The twin evils began to deter vacationers and prompted reform-minded leaders to take over the local government in a series of elections. Although the new leaders did not shut down gambling completely they forced it into the backrooms. Simultaneously, phony therapists, and their drummers, were targeted for extinction. Jacobs survived by sticking to gambling instead of joining the medical quacks, keeping a low profile, regularly paying the necessary bribes and consistently refusing to rig his gaming tables.

After Leo's promise to liberalize the city's risqué entertainment amenities got him elected mayor in 1927, he did not want the resulting gambling to renew the crooked techniques that had previously driven visitors away. Jacobs, Leo decided, was the best candidate to secretly orchestrate the underground community in a way that would reward government officials, boost the local economy, and prevent the covert gaming society from transforming into violent gangs who warred among themselves or cheated their customers with rigged games.

During his term as gambling czar, Jacobs was the major owner of the Southern Club, the Ohio Club and the Belvedere. His keystone was the Southern Club. It had a restaurant on the ground floor and a casino on the second floor and was located across the street from the Arlington Hotel, which normally attracted well-heeled guests. The Ohio was a smaller club located only a block south of the Southern on Central Avenue. It had a street level bar and gaming tables on the second floor. Jacobs opened the Belvedere on forty acres of land about three and a half miles north of downtown on an old highway to Little Rock. Its dining room could seat six hundred people. Although its gaming tables were just off the dining room, people also went to the Belvedere for music and dancing.

Jacobs lived up to McLaughlin's hopes. Employees admitted that the boss immediately fired any worker he caught in a dishonest act. Yet many regarded him as a benevolent father figure. After his death, for example, executors discovered he held a number of unpaid I.O.U.s, including some on police officers. He often hired off duty police and firemen as guards for his clubs. They eagerly sought the part time work because it paid better and was less demanding than their regular jobs.

At times Jacobs would intervene on behalf of the gambling operators. One example involved Chicago gangster Al Capone's attempt to walk away from a gambling debt. Since Capone was often a guest at the nearby Arlington Hotel where he would sometimes book an entire floor of rooms for his gang, he liked to play poker at the Southern Club. He normally entered the club with a fat roll of one hundred-dollar bills but would play with markers (I.O.Us.) if he had run out of cash. On the applicable occasion Al had a bad luck streak and stormed out of the club leaving a stack of unpaid markers. The club management phoned Jacobs who contacted Police Chief Wakelin who contacted Al's brother Ralph. Ralph reportedly told Al that he and his Chicago gang could never return to Hot Springs if Al failed to pay his gambling debts. As a result, Al sent a representative to Jacobs to pay off the markers.[42]

Most of Capone's visits to Hot Springs were during the Prohibition era, especially before 1928 when he bought a South Florida vacation home. While in Hot Springs he enjoyed typical era-specific attractions including the thermal baths, casinos, shooting gallery, horse books, bowling alleys, prostitution homes, pool halls, and golf courses. Although a golf hacker, Al was skilled at pool and liked to play in the billiard room of the Arlington Hotel arcade on rainy days. He normally had an entourage of bodyguards and others in tow and would sometimes book the entire fourth floor of the Arlington. Upon arrival he'd typically send a gang member to the police department to make a $300 donation to their benevolent association.

Since Chicago bootleggers were chronically short of inventory during Prohibition, Capone may have bought some of his supplies from Hot Springs area moonshiners. Although there's no proof of such transactions, government investigators realized that Garland County likely produced more moonshine than was consumed locally. Finally, one Chicago gang member may have tried to assassinate Capone on a highway north of Hot Springs. As Al and his group were driving to a roadhouse beyond the town limits, someone in an overtaking car fired a shotgun into Capone's, but nobody was hurt. While there's no police record of the attack, the gunman that Capone suspected was arrested on unrelated charges in Chicago about a week later. While apparently struggling with the arresting officer, he was shot four times and killed.

Even though Hot Springs' Casino Czar Jacobs insisted that high rollers who could afford to pay their losses make good on their debts, he also wanted the town to avoid getting a reputation of a place where reckless neophytes might be mercilessly bankrupted. In a 1931 *Collier's Weekly* article, Walter Davenport told a story about a stranger who started losing heavily at one of Jacobs' casinos. Under such circumstances Jacobs routinely, but discreetly, inquired into the gambler's background. In this instance he learned that the bettor was a physician with a young family occupying a luxury suite at the town's most expensive hotel. After the plunger had lost $20,000, Jacobs called a halt. He returned $10,000 to the doctor and told the young man to cease gambling anywhere in Hot Springs. When the physician tried to recoup the remaining $10,000 of his losses at other casinos he discovered that the owners would not permit him to make wagers. Czar Jacobs forbade it.[43]

While McLaughlin and Ledgerwood controlled the municipal government, their political Machine also grew tentacles that stretched to other offices. Among them were the district attorneys (DAs) and state circuit court judges applicable to Garland Country. The positions were elected posts. Partly due to its vote-getting capability and possibly due to bribery, the office occupants were tempted to join the McLaughlin Machine. Anyone requesting an investigation into illegal gambling by non-municipal authorities quickly discovered that a grand jury must be assembled to examine the evidence. McLaughlin Machine DAs and circuit judges, however, tended to empanel grand juries composed of members that supported gambling, or to provide jury instructions that were sympathetic to gaming interests.[44]

Fortunately for Owney Madden, Agnes's family had been friendly with the McLaughlins for years. Leo sometimes even joined the Dembys for birthday parties. Owney and Leo also traced their family trees back to Ireland and each was Roman Catholic. The two became friendly. Leo discovered that having a Mafia member in town offered advantages. Owney became both a buffer and communications channel to organized crime. Conversely, Leo's friendship opened doors for Owney after he was permitted to gradually make investments and build businesses in the community following the death of Bill Jacobs in 1940. Eventually, Madden became a minority investor in the Southern Club and Club Belvedere.

Initially, Owney missed New York and regularly walked to the train station to pick up New York newspapers. Since the sounds of the crowds and the bells, whistles, and chugging locomotive pistons reminded him of city life, he tended to remain at the station to read the newspapers. Next he might walk to the Southern Club where FBI agents reported to J. Edgar Hoover that he spent much of his time in the first floor restaurant apparently adapting to retirement.

When, soon after their marriage, he and Agnes attempted to visit friends in Los Angeles, the LA police escorted him to the city limits before he could spend a single night in California. Any trip to New York would likely have ended the same way, if not worse. Owney was exiled to Hot Springs indefinitely, perhaps forever. But, before living in the town a year the underworld called upon him to try to rescue the biggest Mafia leader of the era, Lucky Luciano.[45] .

---

28 James A. Pierce, "From McMath to Rockefeller: Arkansas Governor and Illegal Gambling in Postwar Hot Springs, 1945 – 1970," Thesis for Master's Degree (University of Arkansas, 2008), 8

29 Roy Reed, *Faubus: The Life and Times of an American Prodigal* (Fayetteville, Ark.: University of Arkansas Press, 1997), 319

30 Orval Allbritton, *Leo and Verne* (Hot Springs, Ar.: Garland County Historical Society, 2003), 378

31 *Ibid.*, 319-20

32 *Ibid.*, 389, 566

33 Wendy Richter, "Leo Patrick McLaughlin," *The Encyclopedia of Arkansas History and Culture*. October 15, 2008, available https://goo.gl/DSGJeR [Accessed: July 8, 2017]

34 John William Graves, "Poll Tax," *Encyclopedia of Arkansas History and Culture*, July 10, 2012, available https://goo.gl/jFgmfy [Accessed: July 8, 2017]

35 *Ibid.*; Jim Lester, *A Man For Arkansas* (Little Rock, Ark.: Rose Publishing, 1976), 23

36 Jim Lester, *A Man For Arkansas*, 27-28

37 Orval E. Allbritton, *Leo and Verne*, 300-302

38 *Ibid.*, 305-306

39 *Ibid.*, 251-52, 256; Roy Reed, *Faubus: The Life and Times of an American Prodigal*, 316

40Orval Allbritton, *Leo and Verne*, 127, 260, 263

41 *Ibid.*, 382-84

42 *Ibid.*, 265-72, 314-15

43 Walter Davenport, "Sin Takes a Hot Bath," *Collier's Weekly*, August 8, 1931, 38; Orval Allbritton, *The Mob at the Spa*, 27, 29-30, 33, 38, 62-63

44 Orval Allbritton, *Leo and Verne*, 267

45 Graham Nown, *Arkansas Godfather*, 281-82, 284-85

Chapter Three
Unlucky Stroll

MADDEN WAS NOT the only notorious gangster hounded by the law during the Great Depression. Former bootleggers had to find other income sources after Prohibition ended. Some turned to narcotics, prostitution, and gambling, but one of the biggest opportunities was industrial racketeering. Although traditionally hired as strikebreakers, mobsters increasingly learned that they could extort both the labor and management sides of vulnerable industries. After gaining control of labor unions they could require employers to pay illegal fees to end a strike, or to insure that one was prevented. Conversely, company managements could hire the mobsters as strikebreakers against unions that the hoodlums did not control. After pummeling strikers, mobsters might have sufficiently intimidated the workers to gain control of the applicable union and thereafter extort money from either the union or the companies employing its workers.

Although industrial racketeering increasingly made newspaper headlines, corrupted politicians were reluctant to act. The port of New York was one of the most vulnerable victims. As a matter of economic efficiency, cargo ships needed to be quickly loaded and unloaded. Each ship could ill-afford to stand idle while longshoremen refused to load or remove its cargo. Ship owners were better off simply paying whatever bribes the Longshoremen's Union might demand instead of trying to reach negotiated settlements on a ship-by-ship basis. Normally the illegal fees taken by the unions were large enough to share with corrupt politicians who were thereby motivated to prevent law enforcement interference on the waterfront. The investigation into Brooklyn police corruption that led to New York Mayor O'Dwyer's resignation mentioned in chapter 1 was triggered by just such suspicions.

Finally, in 1935 one New York grand jury had had enough. They demanded a broad industrial racketeering investigation. The designated assistant district attorney tried instead to steer the jury toward scrutinizing local chapters of the Communist Party, which he suggested were responsible. As in the McLaughlin Machine, New York grand juries were often politically controlled. This one, however, became a runaway jury that rejected the Communist conspiracy theory. Despite the assistant DAs efforts to deter them, the jury petitioned the governor to appoint a special prosecutor. As a result, thirty-four-year old Thomas E. Dewey, who would later become a New York governor and twice run for president, was selected to investigate and prosecute New York racketeers.

Thomas E. Dewey | Library of Congress

One reason the governor chose Dewey was because he was in private practice at the time and would presumably have no loyalties to government authorities, many of whom were suspected of corruption. He proved to be an excellent and ambitious prosecutor.

At age twenty-eight—before returning to private practice—Dewey had earlier become the chief assistant to the federal judge assigned to New York's most important federal district. When later recruited from private practice to spearhead the prosecution of racketeering, Dewey assembled a staff of twenty lawyers between the ages of 25 and 40, composed mostly of Harvard or Columbia graduates. He also brought in accountants and a crew of youthful police who were less likely to be corrupted than veterans. Finally, he located his team's offices in a commercial building far from the government facilities where possibly compromised government workers might learn, and pass along, information that could help the suspected criminals.

Despite his best efforts, however, it proved difficult to accumulate enough evidence to charge any notorious mobster with industrial racketeering even though Dewey's team was convinced that many were guilty. They initially targeted Dutch Schultz who had narrowly escaped tax evasion charges that Dewey had prepared against him a couple of years earlier. Schultz unexpectedly beat the tax evasion charge in 1935 by having the trial shifted to a small upstate New York town where he spent liberally at various businesses and gave generously to local charities during the trial.

When Schultz learned that Dewey was coming after him again, but this time for racketeering, he asked Mafia kingpin Lucky Luciano for permission to assassinate Dewey. After Luciano consulted other Mafia leaders, the group concluded that instead of Dewey, it was Schultz who should be executed. They wanted to stop him from killing Dewey because such a murder would trigger unprecedented law enforcement retaliation against the Mafia in general. It would also likely cause corruptible judges to cease cooperating with the Mob. As a result, contract gangsters assassinated Schultz only days before he had hoped to kill Dewey himself.[46]

Schultz's murder forced Dewey to select a second prosecution target. Unfortunately for Luciano, Dewey chose him. It happened almost by accident. One Dewey team member had previously practiced in the women's court where prostitution cases were heard. She noticed that many of the girls used the same bondsmen, which suggested that the city's oldest profession was managed by a structured, although illegal, organization. Partly because the victims were themselves criminals, Dewey was reluctant to expose racketeering within prostitution. Nonetheless, he gave the green light to further investigations.

Gradually the team learned that the girls earned about $300 weekly. Typically, half went to the madam, while $30 was allotted to meals and medical exams. The remaining $120 was left for the prostitutes, which many shared with their pimps. Each madam paid $10 weekly for each employed girl into a fund used to pay lawyers and bondsmen as needed. A total of about 2,000 women were working in about 300 bordellos. Two otherwise insignificant Luciano underlings managed the entire operation. They dropped his name only rarely, such as at times when it might prompt uncooperative participants to pay the required fees.

After a few months Dewey arranged a massive police raid that rounded up about a hundred women. Although judges routinely released them quickly on a $300 bond each—or a $25-each payoff—Dewey was able to get the bonds set at $10,000 this time. As a result, the women remained in jail while Dewey's team questioned them relentlessly to collect additional evidence. Among the male prisoners were bookers and pimps who were threatened with long jail sentences. Ultimately a number of bookers, madams, and prostitutes agreed to testify and finger Luciano as the head of the management organization.

Bathhouse Row | Courtesy of Richard DeSpain

Before Dewey was prepared to spring the indictments he first persuaded the New York State Legislature to change a law that required that only one charge in an indictment could be tried at a time. A new law replacing it allowed multiple charges to be consolidated into a single indictment. That was important for two reasons. First, without it each charge would otherwise need to be tried separately. Second, prostitution's inherent characteristics meant that participants normally commit violations multiple times.

Ultimately Luciano would be arraigned on over ninety counts of compulsory prostitution.[47]

After Lucky had become the greatest among equals within the ring of American Mafia bosses in 1931, he lived like a king. At the time of the Dewey investigation he occupied a $7,000 a year three-room luxury suite under the name of Charles Ross at the Waldorf-Astoria on Park Avenue. He spread money around liberally in order to protect his interests. Among other informants, for example, he paid Waldorf clerks and doormen to alert him whenever unfamiliar persons inquired about either Luciano or Ross. He was alone in the suite one day when a clerk phoned to say that a group of men, possibly detectives, had inquired about Ross and were on the way to the room.

Luciano quickly left the building via a freight elevator with nothing but the clothes on his back. He drove to Philadelphia where he met the local Mafia boss Harry "Nig" Rosen who gave Lucky a Cadillac with Tennessee plates. While in town he bought a new wardrobe and borrowed $25,000 from Rosen.

To the hapless New York police it appeared as though Luciano had simply vanished. Soon police forces launched a multistate manhunt all along the east coast. After learning that he was the target, Lucky drove to Cleveland, left the Cadillac at a train station and bought two tickets for Hot Springs. In order to avoid loneliness while on the lam, he persuaded girlfriend Gay Orlova to meet him in Cleveland and accompany him to Hot Springs. Orlova was a gorgeous Broadway showgirl and Russian immigrant, bold enough about her sex appeal to pose for nude photos in the 1930s.[48]

After arriving in Hot Springs in mid-March 1936, Luciano contacted Owney Madden who introduced him to influential town residents, including potentially helpful law enforcement and other government officials. Among them was Herbert "Dutch" Akers who was the top detective for Police Chief Joe Wakelin. Luciano and Akers quickly became friendly.

Luciano and Orlova settled in for an extended vacation. Sometimes Lucky visited the Central Avenue clubs where he'd place bets with bookies for horses running at Miami's Tropical Park or Chicago's Arlington track. Sometimes he'd gamble at club tables, which might involve taking a seat in poker games that included Nick Dandolos, better known as Nick the Greek. Lucky, however, avoided the marathon sessions that Nick relished.

Later Orlova would join him for evenings of dining and dancing at spots like the Club Belvedere. Owney and Agnes sometimes joined them. New York subordinates phoned Luciano each morning with updates on Dewey, city police activities, general reports on Mafia business and requests for instructions on matters requiring the boss's decision. Afterwards he might take in the morning air with a stroll along a broad walkway known as Bathhouse Row that paralleled Central Avenue.[49]

During one such walk with detective Akers on April Fools' Day the two unexpectedly came across New York detective John Brennan with whom Lucky was personally acquainted. Brennan was in town on another case involving a theft in Yonkers, New York. A widespread wanted poster for the Yonkers thief, displaying pictures of both the man and his pet dog, caught the attention of the Hot Springs police weeks earlier. They soon arrested a visitor fitting the description. Once the detainee was confirmed as the suspect, Brennan went to Hot Springs to return him to New York. While waiting for the extradition papers to be completed, Brennan took a morning walk that resulted in the chance meeting with Luciano and Akers.[50]

As he was walking along Bathhouse Row, Luciano recognized Brennan and asked him what he was doing in Hot Springs, so far from New York. Brennan answered that he was in town to extradite the Yonkers robbery suspect whom, he added, Hot Springs Police Chief Wakelin and detective Akers had arrested. After Akers verified the explanation for Luciano, Brennan asked the New York mobster if he was aware that he was the object of a multistate manhunt triggered by an arrest warrant recently obtained by Dewey. Brennan concluded by asking Luciano to let him take the gangster back to New York along with the suspected Yonkers thief.[51]

Luciano instead asked that Brennan pretend the two of them did not meet while Brennan was in Hot Springs. Brennan replied that he would not do so because if he got caught at the lie he'd lose his job, among other consequences. Before they separated Brennan asked Lucky where he was staying. The Mafia boss answered, "The Arlington." Next Lucky contacted Owney and asked that the latter recommend a lawyer. Owney suggested Richard Ryan.

Brennan pondered his next move. Due to the fact that Lucky was obviously on good terms with local detective Akers, Brennan decided it would be best to inform Dewey's team and let them decide the next move. Since Dewey was out of the office when Brennan phoned, the detective talked to an assistant who recommended that Brennan arrest Luciano immediately but added that the New York cop should get help from the Garland County sheriff. Early that same afternoon Brennan and a deputy sheriff arrested Lucky and took him to the jail at the county courthouse.

Lawyer Ryan quickly filed for a writ of habeas corpus with local chancellor Sam Garrett who ordered that the mobster be released on a $5,000 bond. Madden financed the bond, although he had to do so indirectly because his parole terms required that he not associate with underworld characters. The bond, therefore, was technically provided by the Southern and Belvedere clubs. Since gambling czar Bill Jacobs controlled those clubs the pair's cooperation suggests that Owney was quickly assimilating into the Hot Springs Machine. Thus, Lucky was released the same day he was arrested.

It didn't last. After having issued a 90-count indictment against Lucky, Dewey blew his stack when he learned that the mobster had been released on a trivial $5,000 bail. He held a New York press conference to announce that he could not understand how any judge could set such a low bail unless the magistrate was ignorant of the facts. Dewey amplified his consternation by emphasizing with dismay that Luciano was probably America's most notorious mobster. In telephone calls to Arkansas Governor Junius Futrell and the state's Attorney General Carl Bailey, Dewey added that the New York prosecutors were holding Luciano's top lieutenant on a $75,000 bond and were holding thirty men and eighty prostitutes as witnesses against Luciano.[52]

Governor Futrell phoned Garrett the same day of the writ ruling and ordered that Luciano be brought back into custody. An astonished Garrett sent two deputies sheriff to tell the gangster that his bond was revoked and he must return to jail. Although an irate

Luciano had no choice but to comply, Sheriff Jim Floyd tried to soften the blow. He told Lucky that he could use the sheriff's office for phone calls and even let Gay Orlova visit her jailed boyfriend as often as she wanted. Meanwhile, Dewey told reporters that he had suggested a new bond of $200,000 and was putting one of his aides on a flight to Hot Springs that very night.

While a member of Dewey's team hurried toward Hot Springs, Luciano's top New York lawyer, Moses Pokaloff, was also flying there. Meanwhile Hot Springs city attorney and Ledgerwood law partner, Sonny Davies, joined Luciano's local defense team. They asked for a hearing at Ledgerwood's court that resulted in Luciano's arrest for a lesser charge. They intended that the lesser charge would legally require that Lucky remain in Hot Springs thereby preventing his removal to New York.

When Arkansas State Attorney General Carl Bailey learned of the tactic he travelled to Hot Springs with state rangers to take Luciano to Little Rock. After a local judge ruled against Bailey, the Garland County sheriff took Luciano into custody. Bailey regrouped and arrived before sunup the next day with a dozen heavily armed state rangers. Thus, Luciano was taken to Little Rock under armed guard where he would later appear before a hearing to extradite him to New York.

Three days before the hearing Bailey was visited by a stranger who described himself only as "Charlie's friend." The visitor added that he understood Bailey wanted to become governor in the next election and suggested that a $50,000 campaign contribution might help. Bailey declined the implied offer.

The Little Rock hearing was held on April 6, 1936, before Governor Futrell. After the testimony of several New York witnesses the governor ruled that Charlie's guilt or innocence was not to be decided in Arkansas, but instead in New York. He explained that his only authority was to determine whether Luciano was in New York on the date of the offense specified in Dewey's warrant. Announcing that witnesses answered the pertinent question decisively, the governor signed the extradition papers.[53]

Since a federal court had been involved in moving the hearing to Little Rock, a federal judge—beyond the influence of state officials—granted Charlie's lawyers ten days to file an appeal. Luciano's Little Rock attorney assumed that the ten-day deadline would end on 17 April, whereas it actually ended at midnight 16 April. But state Attorney General Bailey did not mistake the deadline. He asked that a passenger train scheduled to leave Little Rock for St. Louis at midnight be delayed until 12:05 AM so that a heavily guarded Luciano could be put on board. When a connecting train arrived in New York, Dewey greeted Luciano in the company of forty-eight police officers. Two days after the mobster left Little Rock, Carl Bailey announced his campaign for governor of Arkansas and was elected to the office later that year.[54]

Luciano's New York trial lasted about thirty days during May and June 1936. He denied any connection to the two underlings who managed the prostitution business. Unfortunately for him, Dewey had sixty-eight witnesses. Among them were employees of the Waldorf-Astoria who testified that they had seen Charlie in discussions with the two operational subordinates, noted earlier, in his hotel suite. Additionally, telephone records confirmed many conversations between Luciano and the underlings.

One of the prostitutes also testified that she had overhead incriminating conversations when her pimp took her to the hotel room. Another said she had been invited to spend time with Lucky in his bedroom on several occasions and overheard similar conversation prior to retiring to the bedroom. To undermine the gangster's credibility, Dewey forced the obviously wealthy Luciano to admit that he could not explain why his annual tax returns from 1929 to 1935 never reported income of more than $22,500. Finally, the prosecutor forced Lucky to confess his long arrest record and history of association with other well-known gangsters.

Luciano was convicted on sixty-two counts of compulsory prostitution and sentenced to thirty to fifty years in state prison. Since he was not personally involved in overseeing the business, he was stunned by the verdict. His lawyers appealed the case. Despite the fact that three witnesses—including one of the prostitutes who claimed to have overheard incriminating conversations—recanted their testimony, the verdict stood. Dewey rebutted the retractions with evidence that they were perjuries, which Luciano minions obtained by intimidating drug-addicted witnesses. As a result, Lucky was first sent to Sing Sing and then the Clinton prison at Dannemora in upstate New York near the Canadian border. Criminals informally referred to the latter as Siberia.[55]

Even in prison Luciano retained the status of a godfather. Although assigned to work in the prison laundry room, he paid other prisoners to do his work in exchange for gifts. Other men were similarly bribed to clean his cell and perform all his other unpleasant chores that guards assigned to each prisoner. He spent most of his Dannemora time playing cards and strolling around the grounds as other prisoners sought audiences with him. He was still nominally in charge of his Mafia kingdom because, by tradition, a boss's throne could only be relinquished by death or abdication.

Before entering prison, he delegated administrative authority for his Mob family to Frank Costello, who climbed the Mafia ladder via his True Mint Novelty Company, which was a slot machine enterprise hidden under the facade of a candy vending machine operation. Even though in prison, however, Luciano continued to hold ultimate authority.[56]

Shortly after America entered World War II, federal authorities negotiated secretly with Luciano. He was asked to use his influence over the Longshoremen's Union to prevent strikes as well as to detect and combat potential enemy sabotage missions along the waterfront. The unexplained sinking of the French passenger liner *S.S. Normandie* as it was being converted into a troop carrier at Manhattan's pier 88 only a few months after the United States formally entered the war, triggered the discussions.

Luciano agreed to help and tried to negotiate a sentence reduction. The following year he also volunteered to provide contacts in Italy in order to aid the Allied invasion of that country. Although his appeal for a sentence reduction was rejected in 1943, federal officials appreciated his attempts to assist the war effort. After the war ended then-Governor Dewey gave Luciano executive clemency on the condition that he agree to be deported, with the understanding that if he ever returned to the United States he would be treated as an escaped prisoner. On February 10, 1946, Lucky waved goodbye to New York and set sail for Sicily. It was the last time he would see the United States.[57]

Although he never became the central antagonist in a television series like Al Capone in *The Untouchables,* Charles Luciano was as powerful a mobster as any who reached the top of the American underworld. It may be noted, for example, that Frank Costello remained subordinate to Luciano while the latter was in prison even though Costello inspired the Vito Corleone character in Mario Puzo's *The Godfather.* As shall be discussed, Hot Springs also figured-in to Costello's biography.[58]

.

---

46 Thomas Reppetto, *American Mafia,* 164-69

47 *Ibid.,* 174-75

48 Orval E. Allbritton, *The Mob at the Spa,* 75; Selwyn Rabb, *Five Families,* 51

49 Orval Allbritton, *The Mob at the Spa,* 77

50 Beth Bright, "Historian Disappointed by Depiction of Spa City," *Hot Springs Arkansas Sentinel Record* July 9, 2015, available https://goo.gl/CP8xqN [Accessed: July 9, 2017]

51 Martin Gosch and Richard Hammer, *The Last Testament of Lucky Luciano* (New York: Random House, 1981), 194

52 Orval Allbritton, *The Mob at the Spa,* 82-86

53 *Ibid.,* 91-94

54 *Ibid.,* 95-96

55 Thomas Reppetto, *American Mafia,* 176; Selwyn Rabb, *Five Families,* 55-56

56 Selwyn Rabb, *Five Families,* 56-60

57 *Ibid.,* 77-79, 90-91, 114

58 Mark Seal, "The Godfather Wars," *Vanity Fair,* February 4, 2009, available https://goo.gl/wZhG8E [Accessed: July 9, 2017]

Chapter Four
WAR ON CRIME

DURING THE FIRST TWENTY-FIVE years of the bureau's existence, FBI agents were officially prohibited from carrying guns. Additionally, their authority to investigate crimes and apprehend criminals was embarrassingly limited. Everything changed after gangsters massacred one agent and three policemen on June 17, 1933. The next day FBI Director J. Edgar Hoover lifted the firearms ban and sent two machine guns to the agents on the scene. Twelve days later U. S. Attorney General Homer Cummings announced a series of actions to launch a "War on Crime." It was a page one *New York Times* story. Cummings hired a special prosecutor and submitted legislation making it a federal crime to kill a federal agent. In a speech two months later he said, "We are now engaged in a war that threatens the safety of our country—a war with the organized forces of crime." Although the massacre happened in Kansas City, the story began in Hot Springs.[59]

Jelly Nash | Kansas City Police

Two days before the bloodbath forty-six-year-old Frank "Jelly" Nash was a fugitive from the law, holed up in Hot Springs with his new wife Frances and her eight-year-old daughter. His nickname may have resulted from a boyhood fondness for jellybeans, or alternatively for the explosive jelly that the bank robber sometimes used to blow open safes. Although born in Indiana, Nash grew up in Arkansas and Oklahoma small towns where his dad owned hotels. He worked in the hotels until joining the army for three years in 1904 at age seventeen.

After returning from the army he began robbing banks and retail store cash registers but was caught in 1913. The arrest led to a conviction for murder as well as robbery because he had killed an accomplice in order to keep all of the stolen money for himself. Consequently, he was sentenced to a life term at the McAlester, Oklahoma, state penitentiary. After America entered World War I in 1918, Nash smooth-talked his way out of McAlester by volunteering to rejoin the army. His second military term lasted only a few months because the war ended before year-end. Thereafter Nash returned to robberies. After committing a federal offense by stealing U.S. Liberty bonds in a train robbery, Nash fled to Mexico. Eventually, however, he was captured near the border in El Paso and sent to the federal prison at Leavenworth, Kansas, for a twenty-five-year sentence.

Nash's glib talking enabled him to become a prison trusty. Trusties are inmates who are granted more freedom of movement on the prison grounds than other convicts in exchange for performing routine duties under sometimes-too-casual guard supervision. After waiting for the right opportunity, one day Jelly simply walked away from Leavenworth.

He eventually arrived in Chicago where he set-up an illegal Prohibition-era tavern and operated slot machines. He also participated in a variety of robberies with other notorious outlaws such as the Barker Gang and Alvin Karpis, sometimes known as "Ray" to his gang members. By the early 1930s Nash was one of the country's most notorious escapees. Less than a month before the Kansas City massacre he probably helped a group of ten Leavenworth inmates accomplish a spectacular escape. Among them was Harvey Bailey who, uncharacteristically for a violent man, lived to age 91 when he died of natural causes in 1979.[60]

Shortly before the Kansas City killings, Oklahoma City FBI agents Joe Lackey and Frank Smith received a tip that Nash was hidden in Hot Springs. During the early 1930s FBI agents might travel to another city to catch fugitives, but they normally first contacted the local police in order to enlist their help. But in the Nash case the agents were correctly suspicious that the Hot Springs police could not be trusted and might even warn Nash to leave town. While their suspicion might have reflected the town's general reputation, it might also have resulted from a warning by an informant. Therefore, instead of alerting the Hot Springs police, Lackey and Smith contacted Otto Reed, the police chief in McAlester, Oklahoma, where Nash had earlier been imprisoned. Reed habitually followed news reports of Nash's escapades and could identify him on sight.[61]

The trio arrived in Hot Springs by car in on June 16, 1933. They dropped Otto Reed off on Central Avenue while the FBI agents drove up and down the street. Soon Reed emerged from the White Front Cigar Store. The shop was a favorite hangout for visiting gangsters because an underworld character named Dick Galatas managed pool tables and a gambling operation in a back room. Reed motioned the agents to the curb.

After spotting Nash standing near the shop's front door, Reed waited at the curb until the FBI agents drove-up and stopped their car next to him. Reed gestured discreetly toward the man at the store's front door and told the G-men through the car window that the guy was Nash. One of the agents was doubtful because Nash was bald and the suspect had a full head of hair and a mustache. Otto explained that he knew Nash too well to be fooled by a toupee and a new mustache. He was certain they had found their man.

After parking the car the lawmen were ready to enter the store. Even though officially forbidden to carry firearms, all three entered the store with concealed guns. About a dozen patrons were in the front room café where a shotgun was leaning against a wall. Presently, Nash stepped out of the poolroom.

Lackey and Smith pulled guns and trained them on Nash while Reed leveled his pistol at the other patrons, warning them not to interfere. The three put Nash in their car and handcuffed him. When Smith tugged lightly at Nash's hair the toupee came off. Next Smith tried removing the mustache but Nash protested that it was real. He further complained that Smith was handling the expensive toupee too carelessly.[62]

Initially, neither Nash nor anyone in the cigar store realized that Jelly's captors were law enforcement officers. After the car drove away storeowner Galatas phoned the corrupt Hot Springs Chief of Detectives, Dutch Akers. He told Akers that three men in a black sedan had just kidnapped a Chicago businessman named George Miller. Akers, however, knew that "Miller" was merely an alias for Jelly Nash. The detective immediately phoned the police in nearby towns to arrange for roadblocks to stop the getaway car. It was first stopped in the town of Benton where the agents flashed their ID credentials and were waved through. Next Little Rock police stopped it. This time the FBI credentials earned the group a motorcycle escort to the far side of town.

When the group parted ways at the city limits one local policeman asked Nash's captors where they were headed. Although the final destination was the Leavenworth federal prison in Kansas, Lackey named Joplin, Missouri, which was only an intermediate point along the intended route.

After leaving Little Rock, Nash and his captors stopped in nearby Conway at a roadside café. Lackey phoned his Oklahoma City supervisor to report that Nash was in custody. Instead of driving to Joplin through Ozark Mountain back roads, the boss told Lackey to go to Fort Smith on the western border of Arkansas where the group could board an overnight train for Kansas City. Once they arrived in Kansas City the local police would provide an armed caravan to Leavenworth. The train was scheduled to leave Fort Smith at eight-thirty in the evening and arrive in Kansas City at seven the next morning.

The lawmen grew nervous when a stranger looked at them curiously on the Fort Smith station platform. They worried that he might be a gangster sent to rescue Nash. In reality he was an Associated Press (AP) reporter who noticed that Nash was handcuffed. Somebody—no one knows whom—gave the reporter the story. Thirty minutes after leaving the station a six-paragraph report went out to dozens of AP offices, including Hot Springs. It revealed that the captured Nash was headed for Kansas City by train.[63]

Evidently due to a leak among the Little Rock police, somebody told Galatas that Nash was going to Joplin. Galatas phoned a gangland-connected man he knew in Joplin and chartered a private airplane to take Nash's wife and himself there. After Galatas arrived in Joplin somebody phoned him and explained that Nash was instead being taken to Kansas City where he would arrive at the train station at seven the next morning. Frances realized that Nash's Kansas City mobster friend, Verne Miller, might be able to organize a rescue group. Miller also robbed banks, sometimes in the company of Harvey Bailey and others among the group of ten inmates that had recently escaped Leavenworth as explained earlier. When Frances reached Miller by phone he ended the conversation by telling her that he would take care of everything.[64]

The following morning, two Kansas City detectives arrived at Union Station in an armored car intent on taking Nash to Leavenworth. They got out of the car and met two local FBI agents. Soon thereafter a Chevrolet sedan pulled into a nearby parking spot where it faced the FBI agents' two-door car. Miller and two other heavily armed gangsters were in the Chevrolet. When Nash and his captors arrived they walked out to meet the Kansas City lawmen and were directed to the two-door FBI car. Lackey, Smith and Reed slid into the back seat and told Nash to sit in the middle of the front seat. The two local FBI agents planned to sit on either side of Nash.

Suddenly somebody in front of car shouted for everyone in Nash's group to raise their hands high in the air. The four lawmen still standing beside the car were momentarily stunned motionless as their eyes pivoted toward three machine-gun armed men arriving on the scene. From inside the car Frank sensed that his rescuers might mistake him for a lawman and shouted a caution against mistaking his identity. Nonetheless, Miller hollered to his accomplices to open fire and a hail of bullets sprayed the group inside and outside the car.

It was all over in a few seconds as the killers left five men dead in their wake. Among them were Chief Reed, two local police detectives and one of the two local FBI agents. Nash was also killed. Perhaps because of his front seat position and missing toupee, he may have been mistaken for a lawman. But it is also possible that Nash was intentionally murdered in order to prevent him from testifying against various collaborators in his numerous bank robberies. The two FBI agents who arrived with Reed from Hot Springs were wounded, as was a second local agent.

Kansas City newspapers soon printed two killer identity theories. One held that Charles "Pretty Boy" Floyd, a regionally notorious outlaw, arranged the shooting. By coincidence Floyd was earlier involved in a suspicious incident confirming that he arrived in Kansas City the night before the massacre. While Floyd and a sidekick were waiting the previous day for their car to be repaired at a garage near Bolivar, Missouri, the local sheriff recognized the pair and tried to arrest them. But instead they kidnapped the sheriff and drove to Kansas City where they released him unharmed.

Although J. Edgar Hoover preferred to believe the Pretty Boy Floyd conspiracy, a more realistic theory contends that the assassins were Verne Miller and two of the ten inmates who had recently escaped from Leavenworth. Several eyewitnesses identified escapee Harvey Bailey as one of the killers from mug shots. One of the wounded FBI agents likewise identified an Oklahoma bank robber who was among the escapees. While Bailey was never convicted of the slaughter, four months later he received a life sentence for kidnapping a wealthy Oklahoma oilman.[65]

The day after the Kansas City killings Miller unexpectedly arrived in Chicago where he wanted to hide out with a gangster associate. Reports of the massacre were in all the newspapers. Miller told his host that he had a hard time getting out of Kansas City and added that he was consumed with worry that he'd get caught and hanged for two reasons. First, the massacre was front-page news everywhere in the country. Second, he disclosed that he had told Nash's wife over the phone the night before the killings that he would try to rescue her husband. He feared that she would tell the police of their conversation.[66]

The Oklahoma City FBI office discovered a number of suspicious phone calls from Hot Springs to Joplin. As mentioned, the Missouri town was the erroneous destination that Nash's captors provided to the Little Rock police. Further investigation traced phone calls from the applicable Joplin phone number to "Vincent Moore" in Kansas City. The name was an alias for Verne Miller. About five months later Miller's brutally murdered body was discovered in a roadside ditch near Detroit.

Although the identity of a possible FBI informant who might have originally revealed that Nash was holed up in Hot Springs was never officially disclosed, records suggest that it was Dutch Akers. The Hot Springs detective later collected a $500 payment from the Bureau.[67]

Two days after Jelly's killing, a car stopped on the side of the road at an open field fifty miles north of Minnesota's Twin Cities. A blindfolded male passenger got out. He stumbled into the field as the car and driver left. After a few minutes, thirty-eight-year-old William "Bill" Hamm, Jr. removed the blindfold and lumbered to a farmhouse where he phoned his mother in Minneapolis to tell her that his kidnappers had released him uninjured. Bill was the multi-millionaire Board Chairman of the Hamm's Brewing Company. He had been kidnapped by the Barker-Karpis gang upon walking out of his office around noon on June 15, 1933, before being released on a $100,000 ransom four days later.

The Barkers were an outlaw band of sons born to Kate "Ma" Barker. By 1933 only two, Doc and Fred, remained alive or free from prison. Although J. Edgar Hoover liked to refer to the group as the "Ma Barker Gang," Kate actually had nothing to do with the group's escapades, except to spend the money that her sons gave her. Her boys either arranged their exploits themselves or in the company of other bandits such as Alvin "Ray" Karpis or Harvey Bailey. By 1936 twenty-nine-year-old Karpis would rise to be the FBI's Public Enemy Number One and ultimately become the only top-of-list outlaw ever taken alive.

The notorious 1932 kidnapping of aviation pioneer Charles Lindberg's baby in New Jersey probably inspired the 1933 Hamm kidnapping. Despite killing the baby, the Lindberg kidnappers collected a $50,000 ransom. No doubt, the crime's front-page publicity led various bank robbers to suppose that kidnapping might be a less dangerous way to extort large amounts of money.

The Hamm scheme was hatched at a gangland tavern known as the Green Lantern, located at 5451 Wabasha. Much like Hot Springs, St. Paul was a gangster haven. The local police would let criminals stay in the city as long as they checked-in when they arrived, paid the required bribes, and refrained from violence, if not crime. The city's criminal guests ranged from John Dillinger to Bonnie & Clyde. Harry Sawyer, who managed the Lantern, was well connected to the crooked St. Paul police as well as the underworld. Jelly Nash and Harvey Bailey were regular Lantern patrons as were Ray Karpis and the Barker brothers.[68]

The Barkers and Karpis teamed-up in Minneapolis for their first bank job in 1932. They were almost caught because their landlady recognized their "wanted" photos and called the police. Fortunately for the mobsters a corrupt detective delayed a police response long enough for the outlaws to get away. The gang, however, blamed one of their members for attracting the landlady's attention and executed him. Twenty-four-year-old Ray Karpis was already a hardened criminal, having committed his first murder at age thirteen. Doc and Fred Barker were eight and six years older than Ray respectively.[69]

Sometime after the March 1932 Lindberg kidnapping, Lantern manager Harry Sawyer suggested that Karpis try to convince the Barker brothers to join him to attempt a local kidnapping. Two prosperous beer brands were headquartered in the Twin Cities. The Lantern manager knew officers of both companies, including Bill Dunn who was the Vice President of Sales at Hamm and a likely bagman to handle the ransom transfer. After Sawyer added that he could provide a police department mole should the victim's family decide to involve local lawmen, Ray and the Barkers decided to give the plan a try with Bill Hamm.

After grabbing Hamm on the sidewalk as he was leaving his office to go to lunch they forced him into the rear seat of the getaway car and tied a pillowcase over his head. Next they drove to Wisconsin where Hamm signed prepared ransom notes and suggested Bill Dunn as an intermediary. After hearing from the kidnappers, Dunn phoned Bill's brothers who told their mother what was happening. The matriarch insisted on contacting the police.

At the time, only two St. Paul detectives specialized in kidnapping. One was Tom Brown. Unknown to the Hamm family, Brown had agreed to help the gangsters for a $25,000 cut of the proposed $100,000 ransom. As a result, police intervention was fruitless and the Hamm family paid up.[70]

Brown was neither convicted, nor even charged, for his role in the crime although the police department eventually dismissed him as a result of a civil complaint. Thereafter, he earned a living as the proprietor of an Ely, Minnesota, liquor store in a remote part of the state near the Canadian border. Curiously, St. Paul investigators found a Jelly Nash fingerprint on a beer bottle at the house the Barkers had rented while planning the kidnapping. The print, combined with the fact that Verne Miller phoned the Green Lantern the night before his attempted rescue of Jelly in Kansas City, puzzled the FBI. They later learned that Nash had visited the Barkers only a week before the kidnapping.[71]

Since the Hamm adventure paid well and was believed to be less dangerous than bank robbing, six months later Sawyer suggested that the gang try a second target. He proposed Edward Bremer. The thirty-seven-year old Bremer was the heir to St. Paul's Jacob Schmidt Brewing Company fortune. But this time the targeted family differed from the Hamm's in three ways.

First, they were major donors to Franklin D. Roosevelt's successful presidential campaign. Ed's father, Adolph, could have been ambassador to Germany if he had wanted the appointment. Second, the Bremer family was not as wealthy as generally believed. Consequently, the gang asked for more cash than the family had readily available. Third, the family had underworld activities of its own. During Prohibition, for example, the Schmidt brewery supplied the Green Lantern with beer. The Bremers were even rumored to be part owners of the saloon. Moreover, Ed Bremer had purchased untraceable "bearer" bonds at bargain prices from Sawyer who had purchased them from tavern patrons who had previously stolen the bonds. Finally, Ed told his captors that they should have contacted him through Sawyer before selecting him as their victim. He could have, he said, identified wealthier victims and even volunteered the name of a prominent St. Paul railroad executive.

Since the kidnappers overestimated the Bremer wealth, raising the $200,000 ransom took more time than expected. The delay and the Bremer family's attempt to negotiate a lower amount confused the kidnappers. They became increasingly nervous as the unanticipated delays lengthened and publicity mushroomed. Even President Roosevelt spoke angrily about the incident during one of his radio fireside chats. The president mentioned that Bremer was a friend and added that he was not going to let the crime go unpunished. [72]

Partly because of the advantage of having detective Tom Brown as a silent partner, the kidnappers played-out their hand. After three weeks they collected the full $200,000. Karpis took his share and moved to Cleveland where he became head of security at an upscale, but illegal, casino. Although Ray enjoyed the casino job he could not hold it for long because the FBI's Bremer investigation had identified him as a suspect and traced him to Cleveland.

Barely avoiding an FBI raid on his Cleveland bungalow, Karpis traveled to south Florida. Meanwhile, in January 1935 the FBI caught up with the Barkers in Ocala, Florida, in the central part of the state's peninsula. Since that discovery blew Karpis's cover in Miami, he headed for Atlantic City, New Jersey. After a hotel clerk identified his mug photo, the FBI closed in again and Karpis had to shoot his way out of the boardwalk empire. A friend from the Cleveland casino, Freddie Hunter, got Karpis a place to stay at the home of Clayton Hall who was a steel worker at Ohio-based Youngstown Sheet and Tube Company.[73]

Together with Hall, Karpis and Hunter decided to steal Youngstown Sheet's cash payroll on April 25, 1935. They got away with $72,000. Upon dividing the loot, Hunter and Karpis left the area. After loitering a while in Toledo and elsewhere, the pair wandered into Hot Springs in June and remained fugitives there until September. Shortly before they departed the two-faced Dutch Akers held a press conference to say he had discovered that Ray had recently been in town. He provided the FBI with a description of the fugitive's car together with the license plate number. He also gave them the alias names that Karpis and Hunter had been using.

A couple of months later Karpis and Hunter completed a final $34,000 robbery near Cleveland by stealing five bags of registered mail. The two returned to Hot Springs via a chartered airplane. But mail robbery put them on the postal inspector wanted list as well as the FBI list. Akers warned the pair to stay out of the city limits as much as possible since residents were reporting Karpis sightings due to his mug shot on "most wanted" posters scattered around town. As a result, in March 1936 the gangsters moved into a lakefront farmhouse south of town.[74]

Between November 1935 and March 1936 Karpis and Hunter frequently visited a Hot Springs brothel in the Hotel Hatterie. Ray paired off with the Madam, Grace Goldstein (an alias), while Fred hooked up with one of Grace's "girls," Connie Morris. Around Christmastime Karpis gave Goldstein a new Buick that he bought from a dealership owned by Raymond Clinton who would become an uncle to future President Bill Clinton. Together, Karpis and Goldstein visited her family in east Texas. When they returned, she brought along an underage niece to employ at the Hatterie.

By March 1936 postal inspectors had traced the November 1935 Ohio registered mail theft to the steel worker accomplice, Clayton Hall. After interrogating him they followed his Karpis leads to Hot Springs. The investigation deepened as postal inspectors and FBI agents questioned and showed photos of Karpis and Hunter around the town, including to each of Madam Goldstein's girls. Judge Ledgerwood's brother-in-law, Police Chief Joe Wakelin, and Chief Detective Akers grew apprehensive because they were increasingly left uninformed about federal activities. They correctly sensed that the agents suspected the two of double-dealing and generally making Hot Springs a safe haven for Karpis in exchange for bribes. Co-incident to her illegal occupation, Goldstein had her own informants who told her that the feds were hot on her boyfriend's tail. She warned Karpis and Hunter to leave Arkansas.

Back in Youngstown, Hall finally agreed to divulge Karpis's specific Hot Springs address, but only to FBI agents and not postal inspectors. After interrogating Hall, FBI-men set off immediately by air for Hot Springs and arrived on 30 March. In the predawn darkness of April Fools' Day they approached—but did not surround—the house that Hall had specified. At first they could hear the sounds of tenants but everything was quiet by eight o'clock the next morning when they shot tear gas canisters into the house and shouted for Karpis and Hunter to come out. To their surprise the home was empty. The agents would not learn until later that Madam Goldstein and Police Chief Wakelin had left unseen after spending most of the night there wiping the place clean of gangster fingerprints before finishing their time together with a night of sex.[75]

Karpis and Hunter had already fled to New Orleans. On 10 April the FBI flew Hall to Hot Springs from Youngstown. He thought he could get Madam Goldstein to confide Karpis's whereabouts, but she was out of town when he arrived. When she returned two weeks later, detective Akers and Police Chief Wakelin intercepted her. After hours of interrogation they implied they would split the $12,000 reward for capturing Karpis if she would reveal his whereabouts. She cooperated only so far as to say that Karpis was in New Orleans but claimed to be ignorant of the specific address.

Next the Little Rock FBI swooped down and took Madam Goldstein to their office. Since she had visited her family around Christmas together with Karpis they explained that her relatives could be charged for harboring a criminal if she did not cooperate. They added that transporting her niece from Texas to the Hatterie violated the federal Mann Act, which was designed to stop interstate trafficking in prostitution. Eventually she divulged Karpis's New Orleans address as 3343 Canal Street in exchange for a FBI promise to leave her family alone.

####J. Edgar Hoover | Library of Congress#

J. Edgar Hoover flew to New Orleans to take part in the capture because he had been criticized for never having arrested an outlaw himself. Recently a Tennessee senator had embarrassed him with aggressive questioning in front of an appropriations committee where the director's answers disclosed his lack of field experience. Five agents took Karpis and Hunter into custody outside their apartment on 1 May. After the gangsters were well in hand, Hoover stepped out of a hidden spot to confront Karpis face-to-face. The FBI director ever after falsely claimed that he had arrested the Public Enemy Number One personally.[76]

The Bureau's team flew Karpis to St. Paul to stand trial on the kidnapping charge. En route, passengers purchased sandwiches and picked up newspapers when the airliner made a refueling stop in Kansas City. One headline erroneously announced that Karpis had just robbed a Michigan bank. In response the top public enemy wryly remarked to Hoover that he had an airtight alibi for that accusation.[77]

The FBI investigation deepened after Karpis was jailed while J. Edgar Hoover unleashed his administrative wrath. The director had become fed-up with lax law enforcement by local authorities in various cities. He decided to make an example of Hot Springs.

Wakelin, Akers, and Lieutenant Cecil Brock were indicted for conspiracy to harbor Alvin Karpis. The feds cast a legal net over Grace Goldstein as well. In October 1938 the trial began in a Little Rock Federal Court. Over 100 witnesses were prepared to testify but it was all over in twelve days. A jury found Wakelin, Akers, Brock and Goldstein "guilty of harboring Alvin Karpis." Each was given the maximum two-year sentence. Akers was also convicted of protecting another gangster unrelated to the Karpis case. Five months later Goldstein was sentenced at a second trial to an additional five years for taking her underage niece to Hot Springs in order to convert the girl into a prostitute. The persistent prosecution of Goldstein was a response to her attempt to intimidate a juror in the first trial.

Much as Captain Louis Renault in the movie *Casablanca* insincerely professed to be "shocked!...shocked!" to learn that *Rick's Café Americain* included a backroom casino, Goldstein's landlord claimed to be astonished that she had been using the facilities as a brothel for years. Even though he appreciated as a landlord that she paid her rent promptly, he avowed that he would never have permitted her to lease the space had he known of her illegal activities. One older Hot Springs resident who was personally acquainted with the landlord described his denials as "phony."[78]

---

59 Bryan Burrough, *Public Enemies* (New York: Penguin Group, 2004), 52-54, 58

60 Robert Underhill, *Criminals and Folk Heroes* (New York: Algora Publishing, 2015), 20-22 52; Bryan Burrough, Public Enemies, 54

61 Bryan Burrough, *Public Enemies*, 40, 42

62 *Ibid.*, 41-42

63 *Ibid.*, 42-44

64 *Ibid.*, 47

65 *Ibid.*, 48-49, 54-55; Jay Robert Nash, "Who Was Behind the Kansas City Massacre?," *Annals of Crime*, available https://goo.gl/Ndia4G [Accessed: July 9, 2017]

66 Bryan Burrough, *Public Enemies*, 57

67 *Ibid.*, 42, 60

68 Lauren Peck, "Abducted in St. Paul!," *Minnesota Good Age*, June 13, 2016, available https://goo.gl/4fzcE4 [Accessed: July 8, 2017]; "Ma Barker," The Spell of the West, available https://goo.gl/HL2KfX [Accessed: July 9, 2017]; William Helmer and Rick Mattix, *Public Enemies: America's Criminal Past 1919-1940* (New York: Checkmark Books, 1998), 153

69 Bryan Burrough, *Public Enemies*, 34-35

70 *Ibid.*, 36-37, 109

71 *Ibid.*, 60, 549

72 *Ibid.*, 192, 194, 196, 198,

73 *Ibid.*, 197, 431, 494, 510, 514, 522

74 *Ibid.*, 525-28; Orval Allbritton, *Leo and Verne*, 336

75 Orval Allbritton, *Leo and Verne*, 338-39; Bryan Burrough, *Public Enemies*, 532-33

76 Bryan Burrough, *Public Enemies*, 536-39; Don Whitehead, *The FBI Story* (New York: Random House, 1956), 108; Jane Turzillo, "Hot Springs Madam Harbored Public Enemy Number 1," *Dark Hearted Women*, September 24, 2012, available https://goo.gl/1tksef [Accessed: July 9, 2017]

77 Don Whitehead, *The FBI Story*, 109

78 Orval Allbritton, *Leo and Verne*, 340-4; Don Whitehead, *The FBI Story*, 107-8

Chapter Five
LEO AND VERNE

LEO MCLAUGHLIN AND VERNE LEDGERWOOD were born about a year apart in 1888 and 1889, respectively. McLaughlin lived in Hot Springs all his life and Verne moved to the town with his Kansas parents only a couple of months after he was born. Originally, Leo's dad owned a grocery and feed business as well as rental properties. Later, at the prompting of Leo's oldest brother, the McLaughlins founded a hardware store. Verne's dad and two uncles opened a bakery shortly after arriving in town. But their big break came after the turn of the century when Verne's dad and uncles formed a partnership that became the local bottler and distributor for the then nascent Coca-Cola Company.

Coca Cola Ad | Library of Congress

Although the boys probably knew each other earlier, they certainly became acquainted by 1904 when they were classmates at the town's Central School. Like other boys of the era, Leo and Verne were expected to work when not in school, especially on Saturdays. But unlike most of the other boys they worked in their family businesses. Since Leo loved horses all his life he liked to make grocery deliveries. Verne enjoyed managing the bottling equipment but would deliver baked goods when required. Leo had three brothers and two sisters while Verne had a single, older brother.[79]

At a time when Arkansas boys often left school to join the workforce years before earning a diploma, Leo and Verne were two of only four boys in their 1907 high school senior class that included eighteen girls. Leo's two older brothers, for example, went to work in the family business without ever graduating from high school. Although Leo was the senior class president, Verne was the more ambitious and the better student. In an era when most Arkansas lawyers gained their credentials by apprenticing to older attorneys, he wanted to earn a college law degree. Both played football while in high school. Verne was the quarterback and Leo was recognized as one of the best fullbacks in the state. They also played on the school's first basketball team.

Both were popular with girls. As a senior Verne fell in love with a freshman named Bess Wakelin, whom he would marry. On a dare, Bess first got his attention by running by him at lunch and swiping his hat. He chased after her and said he would paddle her if she did it again. When she repeated the stunt a few days later, Verne was good to his word and paddled her before twenty or thirty students. Although the act was evidently considered playful and not sexually harassing, Verne's mom was displeased when she heard the story. She told him to apologize to Bess and bring Wakelin home so that she could meet the girl. After the visit Verne's mother told her son that he should not feel a need to become involved with other girls or let Bess walk out of his life because she was the right girl for him to eventually marry.

As they approached graduation, Leo confided to Verne that he wanted to avoid going to work in his dad's grocery, feed, and hardware business. Verne suggested that the two of them attend the University of Arkansas as roommates. The school was in Fayetteville, which is about 200 miles from Hot Springs. Leo explained that he planned to attend the state university for a single year and then transfer to Tulane University in New Orleans to earn a law degree.[80]

Since they only intended to study at the University of Arkansas for a single year the pair enrolled as "special students." Leo got homesick and dropped out after only two weeks. Although missing his hometown, Leo wanted to avoid working in the family business. Before leaving Fayetteville, he told Verne that he might try getting involved in politics when he returned to Hot Springs.

Verne warned that if he returned to Hot Springs after only two weeks in college Leo might never earn an official university diploma. But Leo demurred, saying that he could get an education later. Characteristically, Leo never thereafter even attended college although later political biographies would describe him as a University of Arkansas law graduate.[81]

Allen "Sonny" Davies, who was a year-younger high school classmate, triggered Verne's interest in Tulane. They shared youthful ambitions to become attorneys and even decided they'd like to eventually become law partners. Davies had an aunt who lived near the Tulane campus. When he wrote her of his desire to attend the school with Verne, she invited both to live with her after they enrolled in 1908. For the next four years Verne studied conscientiously and became a leader within the various study groups that are characteristic of law school. His romantic attachment to Bess Wakelin back in Hot Springs evidently helped keep Verne focused on his studies.

Ledgerwood graduated second in his class and Tulane's dean tried to recruit him into the school's faculty. The dean suggested that Verne first burnish his credentials with extra study at an eastern university before returning to New Orleans. Instead, Verne followed his original plans. He set up a law practice in Hot Springs and admitted Sonny Davies as a partner the following spring.[82]

When Leo abruptly returned to Hot Springs after only two weeks at university, his dad insisted that he work in the family business. Since his sojourn to Fayetteville was designed to prevent such a fate, Leo told his dad that he intended to become a lawyer by apprenticeship. He selected attorney George P. Whittington as his mentor. Whittington was a fine lawyer with a degree from the University of Virginia. He was also the grandson of Hiram Whittington who was one of the first Hot Springs settlers. But apprenticeship was only the first step in the process that Leo was selecting to become a lawyer. Eventually, he would need to pass the Arkansas Bar exam.

Leo soon proved that his parting comments to Verne at Fayetteville about wanting to enter politics were not empty words. In 1910 Whittington shrewdly observed that an informal settlement of a temporary convulsion in the Garland County Democratic party might present a favorable opportunity to gain a political ally. As a member of the Arkansas state House of Representatives, he sensed that Leo might also be able to get elected and become that ally, despite being only twenty-two years old.

Leo's campaign supported a proposition—then popular in Hot Springs—that would allow each county to vote on prohibition within its own borders as opposed to a competing proposition that would mandate uniformity throughout Arkansas after a statewide vote. In 1915 Leo's viewpoint prevailed when the state adopted the local option alternative. By accompanying Whittington on the campaign trail the budding politician learned enough about electioneering to win and even got a few more votes than his mentor. Both were admitted to the next legislature because the two available seats in the district were assigned to the two top vote getters, which turned out to be McLaughlin and Whittington, respectively.

After the legislative session ended in May 1911, Leo returned to Hot Springs and rented an office next to Whittington's. He put a sign on the door proclaiming that it opened into the offices of Leo P. McLaughlin, Attorney at Law.

Leo would maintain an office in the building for the next forty years. Although he practiced as a lawyer, there is no record to confirm that he was entitled to do so. From approximately 1900 to 1940 University of Arkansas law graduates were automatically admitted to the state bar. As noted, however, Leo never graduated from the school. Those who were not U-of-A graduates during the era could legally become lawyers by taking an oral exam before the state's supreme court, but there is no record that McLaughlin ever passed such an exam.[83]

The years before Leo was elected Hot Springs mayor in 1927 were an era of lenient credentials enforcement within the Arkansas legal community. Since the impeccably qualified Whittington sometimes gave Leo overflow assignments, however, the older lawyer's implied endorsement was good enough to get the younger man's law practice underway without a credentials challenge. Nonetheless, even though Whittington would typically introduce McLaughlin as a personal associate the pair never had an official partnership. Once Leo's business became self-propelling he apparently never even tried to obtain the required qualifications. After he became mayor all sensible citizens realized it was too dangerous to question his background because of his power to punish those who tried to upset his apple cart in most any context.[84]

In the spring of 1912 Leo won an election to become the Hot Springs City Attorney and was the youngest to ever hold the post. Illegal gambling was wide open at the time. There was no organized control, not even informally. Each casino made its own bribery deal with the applicable politicos and law enforcement officers. At the urging of out of town visitors, however, a 1913 grand jury investigation revealed widespread corruption.

A wealthy Indiana visitor named Frank Fox indirectly triggered the investigation after he became the $20,000 victim of a con game. Among Fox's friends was William J. Burns, the founder of the famous Burns Detective Agency. Fox hired the agency to investigate his complaint. Burns collected enough evidence to prompt the local prosecuting attorney to pursue the case, which led to a number of spectacular arrests including one that resulted in a wild chase down Chicago's Michigan Avenue.

Hot Springs's reputation suffered as the enquiry started making headlines in newspapers across the nation. Civic leaders decided it was time for Hot Springs to clean up its act if the town was to survive as a resort destination. Even though backed by prosperous gambling interests, the incumbent mayor was only able to win the Democratic primary by ten votes. Nonetheless, that victory should have enabled him to take the November general election because of Arkansas's traditional one-party political structure. But 1913 was not to be a normal political year.

Dr. Jacob McClendon, a respected local physician, agreed to be an independent mayoral candidate in the general election. Much to the anguish of the gambling interests, he won. He shut down the wagering clubs and declared war on con artists. Under the influence of the growing reform sentiment, Verne Ledgerwood was appointed police judge after the previous elected officeholder died. With his confidence boosted by the appointment, Verne married Bess Wakelin a few months later. He was twenty-four and she was twenty.

Later that year Hot Springs suffered a devastating fire. Prominent businesses, such as the Ledgerwood Coca-Cola bottling franchise, would rebuild although sometimes under altered ownership. For example, one of Verne's uncles sold his interest in the franchise to his brothers and left Hot Springs for good. He ended-up moving to the Los Angeles area where he had the good fortune to become the Coca-Cola bottler in his new hometown. But many weaker businesses never rebuilt.

When Verne became police judge the office was merely a part time appointment. He would normally attend to it in the morning and return to his private law practice with Sonny Davies in the afternoon. But after Davies was elected to the Arkansas state legislature he pushed through a bill that transformed the city's police judge into a municipal judge, a full-time position.[85]

By 1915 twenty-seven-year-old McLaughlin had become arrogant through his status as city attorney. He became overly proud to be a rising young politico, emerging community leader, and member of a prosperous and established family. That year a reputable New York developer, knowledgeable of European spa centers, proposed a fourteen-acre sanitarium for downtown Hot Springs. Since the town's population was then only about 15,000 the project was large enough to have had a big favorable impact on the community's future.

The design included a clinic that could accommodate six hundred guests. It also included an adjacent eight-story hotel. All local property owners, except one, agreed to sell the required land. The exception was Leo's mother who had inherited the property after her husband died in 1912. Although she supported the project, she told the civic leaders to negotiate with her son. Leo delayed and repeatedly tried to increase the sales price by various tactics, including an unlikely claim that he had a higher offer from another buyer.

Eventually, the project's local proponents wrote Leo's mother directly explaining her son's stubbornness. A local newspaper cited the letter in a two-column story about the delays affecting the development. Leo's mom exploded with anger and humiliation, primarily directed at her son. She quickly signed an agreement to option her land to the project. Unfortunately, the out of state financiers rejected her version of the document and soon thereafter

Hot Springs Promenade – 1910 | Library of Congress

turned their attentions toward business proposals elsewhere that profited from the growing European war.

After the sanitarium debacle many voters soured on McLaughlin. Nonetheless, perhaps by selectively bestowing the favors available from his office, in December 1915 he won enough votes to be re-nominated as the Democratic candidate for city attorney. One way he may have gained support with certain influential voters was to settle cases in which fines were assessed at the police court. As city attorney he settled over half of the police court appeals that would otherwise have landed in the state circuit court. Presumably his settlements reduced the fines levied by the police court, which encouraged defendants to abandon any efforts to appeal. Thus, Leo was surprised when a youthful challenger, Sam McConnell, ran against him and won in the 1916 general election for city attorney. It would be the last time he'd lose an election. [86]

Meanwhile a group of leading physicians formed a secret committee to rid the town of medical quacks and their aggressive promoters, termed drummers. The drummers typically greeted visitors at the local train station, or even the stations in Little Rock and Memphis, in an effort to waylay new patients for the drummer's physician clients. The committee hired William Bouic as their lawyer, who also happened to be an assistant prosecuting attorney.

Bouic recommended a sting operation. He planned to catch drummers as they confessed their activities to someone they presumed to be a trusted advisor. Partly because the two had adjacent offices, Bouic approached McLaughlin to be the trusted confessor. Even though Leo had previously defended drummers, he switched sides for a larger fee.

The Burns Agency installed a hidden microphone in Leo's office and connected it to a receiver in Bouic's office. Over the next several weeks Leo asked some of his previous clients to meet at his office under the pretext of needing specifics about how the drummers conducted their practice. He encouraged them to elaborate by pointing out that a bill affecting their business was presently under consideration by the state legislature. He thereby learned the identity of their clients, how they were paid, who paid them and the general pattern of drumming operations.

Attorney Bouic also hired Gabby Carter as an undercover operative. Carter got a job as a hotel manager where he drummed-up patients for participating client doctors. Unfortunately for Carter it soon became apparent that many licensed doctors—as opposed to quacks—also paid drummers. When the anti-drumming committee asked those doctors to provide donations to pay for the investigation, Carter's cover was blown. That prompted one of the physicians who had engaged Carter as a drummer to request a private meeting. But the meeting was not private. Several sinister men accompanied the doctor. Under gunpoint they forced Carter to sign papers revoking his earlier affidavits, which had summarized his drumming activities and findings.

After signing the papers, his captors rushed Carter off to New Orleans. Since they were aware that he was previously a drug addict they tried to re-addict him by providing a steady supply of morphine on the train ride south. Before they could complete their plan to send him to Cuba where they hoped the anti-drumming committee would not be able to find him, Carter escaped and phoned Bouic in Hot Springs. Bouic phoned a Hot Springs native who was then a New Orleans doctor. The New Orleans doctor gave Carter a safe haven until Carter's evidence was presented to a Hot Spring grand jury. The sting led to a successful prosecution of twenty-three physicians, some of them previously prominent citizens. Leo participated in the action.[87]

By 1917 drumming had vanished from Hot Springs and gambling was sharply reduced. While the reforms improved the resort's image they also curtailed the local economy, as did the 1913 fire. Consequently, the town's population declined from 14,000 in 1910 to 10,000 in 1920.

As American enlistments for World War I burgeoned in the second half of 1917, Leo tried to avoid military service. He hoped that he might gain a draft exemption by winning the 1918 city attorney election. He reasoned that incumbent McConnell was vulnerable for a couple of reasons. First, when the mayor tried to protect the city treasury by vetoing an overpriced street paving contract, McConnell informed the city Commissioners that they could override it, which they did. Thus, McConnell had turned the mayor into an enemy. Second, McConnell was a Republican at a time when Arkansas voters would normally elect members of the GOP only under the most compelling circumstances.

Leo turned out to be half right. He won the election, but the draft board would not grant him an exemption. His solution was to assume the dubious authority to appoint his temporary replacement, Orlando Sumpter, with a private understanding that Sumpter would return the office to Leo when the latter was discharged from the Army.

After Leo joined the Army in May 1918, he was at a Louisiana boot camp less than a month when he married a Hot Springs girl he had been dating without his mother's knowledge. Together with one of his sisters, Leo's mother went to Louisiana to try and get the marriage annulled. Mother McLaughlin, a devout Roman Catholic, was determined to veto the marriage plans of any of her children when she considered the presumed spouse to be unsuitable. Due partly to their mother's tight control, her daughters never married. Mother McLaughlin—who controlled the family purse strings—somehow legally erased Leo's marriage. After about a year his ex-wife returned briefly to Hot Springs as a performer in a theatrical group that identified her in the program by her maiden name.

Next Leo feigned insanity and was sent to a base hospital. After a doctor diagnosed the illness as phony Leo was forced to leave the hospital and returned to his infantry unit in July. The next month he was on a troopship to France.

The war ended in November, before his battalion reached the battlefront. Since his unit was assigned to occupation duty, Leo did not return to Hot Springs until April 1919. About two months later McLaughlin resumed his post as city attorney and started to compile a favorable performance record. During the next year he tried lawsuits for the city and was successful in all but one. He also convinced the privately-owned water company to improve its facilities, thereby saving Hot Springs residents about $75,000 annually in fire insurance premiums.[88]

Thus, when measured by on-the-job performance, Leo appeared to be in good shape to win reelection as city attorney in 1920. But the day after he filed, a local lawyer with degrees from Vanderbilt and the University of Texas announced that he would challenge Leo. Moreover, a festering disagreement over fees that Orlando Sumpter claimed Leo owed him for legal work a few years earlier prompted Sumpter to also run against Leo.

Leo felt betrayed by Sumpter's decision because he had earlier appointed Sumpter as a mere placeholder to the city attorney post while Leo was in the Army. Moreover, since most informed voters knew of the Sumpter-McClaughlin feud, the Vanderbilt-graduate candidate looked silly when he publicly accused the pair of teaming up against him. Consequently, the knowledgeable newspapers and political leaders rejected the newcomer and lined up behind Leo whom they also favored over Sumpter due to the latter's objectionable personality. As a result, Leo handily won reelection.[89]

Thereafter, Leo fulfilled his city attorney duties competently, if not exceptionally. His private law practice consisted of divorce and other cases that did not often require trials. Despite the fact that he never acquired the proper licenses everyone seemed to be unaware of it. They accepted his business as legitimate out of force of habit. Nonetheless, his willingness to practice law without a license was an additional clue to Leo's sinister side. Another unsavory episode in 1922 that also revealed his dark side received little public notice until his 1927 mayoral campaign.

In 1922 an elderly and ill Kansan, Thomas Cosgrove, arrived in Hot Springs hoping to improve his infirmities and prolong his life through hydrotherapy. Since Cosgrove was a stranger in the town, and evidently had no family, he wanted help arranging his affairs. He asked the priest at St. Mary's Roman Catholic Church for a recommendation. The priest recommended Leo who was a parishioner. Cosgrove met trustingly at Leo's office where he disclosed that he bequeathed all of his property, including $45,000 in Liberty Bonds, to a Kansas orphanage. He wanted Leo to look after him, pay his bills, and tend to his affairs during his last days. Leo wrote-up an agreement that Cosgrove signed, probably without fully understanding.

The contract empowered Leo to use Cosgrove's money for the latter's care and welfare. In exchange Leo would receive any money or bonds remaining after Cosgrove died, which happened shortly thereafter. After the body was shipped back to Kansas, Leo relied upon the contract to make a $42,500 claim on the estate. When the

Kansas orphanage produced the will, Leo would not budge. He may have assumed that the orphanage would file suit in a local Hot Springs court, where Leo calculated on getting a home field advantage. Instead the orphanage filed their suit in federal court. The case prompted Leo to compromise. He offered a settlement in which he and the orphanage would evenly divide the $42,500. Rather than pay the legal fees for an uncertain trial, the orphanage accepted the compromise.[90]

A few days after Leo won the 1927 mayoral election he and Verne invited other officeholders to a meeting in the civic auditorium. They distributed the invitations in a manner that gave each recipient the impression that he was a member of a select group of invitees. The resulting meeting was the beginning of the McLaughlin Machine. Leo and Verne explained that if each of the department heads and their employees voted as a block they would strengthen the power of the incumbents, who were urged to thereafter hire nobody that would fail to back Machine candidates. All employees were advised to have poll tax receipts for themselves, spouses, and other family members.

The pair further explained how they planned to relax gambling restrictions. Officeholders who played along with Leo's administration would receive "donations" from casino owners for helping to keep them open. At the end of the meeting Leo's plan was fully accepted.

Next, Leo asked the city council—analogous to a municipal Board of Directors—to caucus in Judge Ledgerwood's office. Little is known of what was actually said, but the message was much like the one given to the department heads at the civic auditorium. As a result, seven of the sixteen aldermen would thereafter remain part of Leo's Machine during its entire twenty-year life. Of the remaining nine, those who declined to cooperate with Leo were gradually defeated at the polls. Eventually, members of the council merely rubber-stamped Leo's initiatives and did not truly represent their wards. After Leo was inaugurated as mayor, Verne's law partner, Sonny Davies, was sworn-in as Leo's replacement for city attorney. The Machine was rapidly assembling.[91]

About four years after Leo was elected mayor, Walter Davenport of *Collier's Weekly* wrote the magazine's monthly profile article about Hot Springs. Davenport was impressed with "the simplicity of [the town's] one-man government." He wrote, "The name of this one-man government is Leo P. McLaughlin. He is the head of the police. He runs the fire department. He decides whether streets should be paved ... Mr. McLaughlin appears to be the whole government machine and I found nobody with proof to the contrary." At the time the town had only 16,000 residents but annually hosted about 250,000 vacationers. Davenport admitted to his readers across the nation that Leo financed the municipality chiefly by collecting fines from the profits of casino operators. "Make the visitor pay," said Leo, "but give him so much fun that he forgets the price."[92]

---

79 Orval Allbritton, *Leo and Verne*, 12, 26-27

80 *Ibid.*, 31-34

81 *Ibid.*, 36, 56

82 *Ibid.*, 37, 56

83 *Ibid.*, 55, 89

84 *Ibid.*, 56

85 *Ibid.*, 58, 60-61, 64-65, 68, 75, 77, 84, 90

86 *Ibid.*, 94-96, 100-101

87 *Ibid.*, 115-120

88 *Ibid.*, 136-37, 144-46, 150-51, 166, 188

89 *Ibid.*, 192

90 *Ibid.*, 252-53

91 *Ibid.*, 261-63

92 Walter Davenport, "Sin Takes a Hot Bath," *Colliers Weekly*, August 8, 1931, 10-11

Chapter Six
MACHINE POLITICS

HISTORY TEACHES THAT until a new ruler has either destroyed all his rivals, or wins them over to his side, someone from the old regime will ultimately challenge his authority. The first test for Leo's Machine came with the 1928 Democratic Party primary. Contrary to the unspoken understanding that Machine candidates would not oppose one another, city clerk Fred Fowler announced that he would seek the office of county tax collector against George Leatherman. Fowler was annoyed with Leo because he had worked hard for the mayor's election the preceding year presuming that he and Leo had an understanding that Fowler would be appointed police chief upon Leo's election. As noted, however, the post went to Judge Ledgerwood's brother-in-law, Joe Wakelin, due to an identical, but conflicting, understanding between Leo and the judge.

After conferring with Ledgerwood about Fowler's announcement, Leo and Verne decided that they would publicly take no action against him other than to say that Leatherman was the administration's candidate. But shortly before the election they distributed mock ballots to Machine members, indicating the favored candidate for each office. Fred's name had a bold black mark scratched through it. As a result, Leatherman beat Fowler by more than a two-to-one margin in the August primary.[93]

Meanwhile Leo sensed a brush fire of resistance among the old guard in the police department when Chief of Detectives, Green

Brown, outspokenly criticized the administration. Leo promptly fired Brown and replaced him with Dutch Akers. As noted, Akers would later serve jail time for aiding Public Enemy Number One, Alvin "Ray" Karpis, but Akers already had a shady reputation when Leo chose him to replace Brown. He had, for example, a dubious connection to a ring of car thieves. In one instance when a guest at the Arlington Hotel complained to the desk clerk that his car was missing from its parking spot, the clerk suggested that he contact detective Akers. The clerk further suggested that the guest offer Akers a fifty-dollar reward to "find" the car. The lodger walked to the police department and did as instructed. By the time he arrived back at the hotel the car had been returned.

Similar stories underscored Akers's dubious reputation. When hotel guests asked clerks for advice about where to buy firearms, for example, they were sometimes told to contact detective Akers who held an inventory of confiscated weapons. He would sell the guns and keep the proceeds. Similarly, prostitutes learned that Dutch was a source of bargain priced jewelry, also evidently confiscated. Finally, he was once arrested on a federal liquor law violation during an earlier job as a railroad detective.

But from another perspective Akers fit the stereotypical image of the era—inculcated by Hollywood—of a shrewd detective who benefitted from a touch of the reformed outlaw in his background. Akers could, for example, often spot suspicious characters on site. He would sometimes meet the arriving trains to scan the unloading passengers in order to identify undesirables. When he spotted anyone that he suspected of being a confidence man he'd greet him by saying, "It's nice to see you. For your information there's a train leaving in a couple of hours. Be sure and be on it." But Akers was most valuable to Mayor McLaughlin as an informant. Although Leo had moles in every department, Dutch became one of the most effective. Leo's younger brother George assured Dutch's loyalty to the mayor by attaching himself to the detective as a frequent companion.[94]

When Leo got word in 1929 that city engineer Cleveland Smith planned to run against him for mayor, McLaughlin promptly relieved the engineer of his duties. Fred Fowler's wife, who was also a city employee, urged her husband to back Smith. Nonetheless, before long all sixteen aldermen endorsed Leo. Smith countered by disclosing an alleged incident in which Leo's Machine partners, Police Chief Wakelin and detective Akers, encouraged a prisoner to bribe them. When the prisoner explained that he would not pay the bribe because it would not leave him enough money to pay his fine, the two officers allegedly got the fine reduced. Smith relied upon a Fred Fowler affidavit to document the suspicious fine reduction.

Politically, Fred's affidavit was a fatal mistake. Leo defeated Smith by a three-to-one margin. Afterward Leo took his revenge on the Fowlers. Although he could not fire Fred because Fred held an elective post, he fired Fred's wife, Clara. She, in turn, was overcome with anger. Armed with a pistol, she confronted a woman suspected of harassing her with anonymous political phone calls during Smith's election campaign. In the heat of argument Clara fired a wild shot that ricocheted off a wall and struck a bystander a glancing blow. Clara was immediately remorseful and hurried the wounded person to a doctor.

Meanwhile someone phoned the police, which prompted some officers to go to the doctor's office and arrest Clara. An unknown person at the police department also notified Fred, who hurried to the doctor's office with a pistol in hand. Fred disarmed the arresting officers, sent them on their way and said that he would take his wife to the police station himself. Instead, he surrendered her to a local constable who escorted the pair to a bond hearing. After Clara was released under bond, Fred took her to a Little Rock hotel for the night to give tempers in Hot Springs time to cool down.

Overnight, however, a fire broke out in Fred's office. Leo immediately suggested arson as the cause. He explained that Fred's department was in the middle of an audit and implied that Fowler had destroyed evidence. Although the accounting firm explained that the nearly completed audit failed to disclose any irregularities, Leo was not satisfied. He hinted that the auditors should "look again" if they wanted to win any more contracts from the city of Hot Springs. Ultimately Fred was charged with embezzlement of about $3,000 but the case was so weak that the jury deliberated less than an hour before rendering a not guilty verdict.

Fred Fowler's tribulations together with the firings of Green Brown, Cleveland Smith and Fred's wife were compelling warnings to anyone who might contemplate challenging the McLaughlin Machine. As Fowler's defense attorney put it, "The real grievance against him [Fowler] is that he is not in harmony with the city administration."[95]

Although the experiences of Brown, Smith, and Fowler convinced Machine insiders that it would be futile to oppose Mayor McLaughlin, some outsiders had yet to learn the lesson. In 1933 the owner of a lumberyard, E. R. Boll, announced plans to run against Leo. Unfortunately, Boll's business was dependent upon three major road construction contractors for Hot Springs and Garland County. After two of the road builders told Boll that they would no longer buy his lumber or building supplies, he withdrew from the race. Soon thereafter Boll's business went bust after a large order for bridge timbers was cancelled. He and his family moved about seventy miles away to Pine Bluff where the best job he could get was that of night watchman. It was quite a fall for a previously well-off business owner.

Central Avenue - 1935 | Courtesy of Garland County Historical Society

The following year a former member of the Arkansas House of Representative, Jay Rowland, decided to challenge the Machine's circuit judge candidate, Earl Witt. Although one weekly newspaper tried to help Rowland by accusing Witt of alcoholism and accepting bribes from gambling interests, Witt won the election anyway. When Rowland next ran directly against Leo for the mayor's office in 1937, he lost by a twenty-to-one margin. Eventually Rowland joined the Machine by replacing Sonny Davies as city attorney who resigned due to illness. Once in his new post, however, Rowland participated in a municipal bond kickback scheme that cost the city thousands of dollars.

The 1936 Garland County Sheriff's election demonstrated that the political Machine's power extended even to the state courts. After the previous sheriff retired, three men filed for the post. The Machine candidate won with about five thousand votes as compared to a combined two thousand for the other two candidates. The second-place finisher filed suit, claiming that the Leo's candidate received over four thousand votes from holders of fraudulent poll tax receipts. Many of the holders, for example, had been transitory workers at the Oaklawn Park horse race track, which was then in season for only about a single month per year. State circuit court Judge Earl Witt dismissed the case partly on the technicality that it failed to include the third-place finisher as a party to the suit. An appeal to the state Supreme Court upheld Witt's ruling on the same technicality.

Although nobody could foresee it at the time, however, the Machine made a fatal error in 1937. The state's new governor, Carl Bailey, was hostile toward Hot Springs politicos because they defied him during the Lucy Luciano episode a year earlier. Soon after his inauguration Bailey sent four squads of state troopers into Hot Springs with warrants to search, seize, and destroy gambling equipment. They hit all of the major clubs and casinos. It was a major setback that compelled Leo and Verne to travel to Little Rock, hats-in-hands, to meet the governor face to face. After some awkward moments they sensed that Bailey had political ambitions beyond the governor's office.

Verne said, "Governor, you may want to run for a higher office some day and we can help you. Our friends in the gambling industry are willing to provide campaign support for a candidate who is friendly to Hot Springs."

As Bailey paused to ponder the point Leo added, "And we can guarantee delivery of the Garland County vote in the next election. You would not want to throw that away."

A few days later the town's bookies, clubs, and casinos were back in operation. When an anti-gambling delegation visited the governor to report that illegal gaming had restarted in Hot Springs he told them that they should take their complaint to the local courts.

A few months later Leo got an opportunity to demonstrate his commitment to Bailey. When Arkansas senator Joseph T. Robinson died in office during the summer of 1937 Bailey wanted the vacant post. In support, Leo moved at a state Democratic Party meeting that Bailey be nominated to fill Robinson's seat. Not only did the motion carry, but it stipulated that the nomination was to be "without opposition," thereby preventing any other Democrat from seeking the Senate seat. A number of Party leaders, including future Senator John L. McClellan, criticized the action. They preferred Congressman John Miller who was forced to campaign as a political independent but won the election anyway. Nine years later Miller would be a U.S. District Court judge when he would make a key voter fraud ruling against the McLaughlin Machine.[96]

In 1938, nine years after Leo beat Cleveland Smith in the former's reelection, Smith's brother Brad was killed by a gunshot wound. Brad and Cleveland were partners in a construction business. Each was regarded as *persona non grata* around city hall. The Smith Brothers Construction Company, for example, seldom won contracts from either the city or the county during the McLaughlin era. One investigation suggested that Brad committed suicide but even the city coroner rejected that opinion and concluded that Brad was murdered. Both a coroner's jury and a grand jury came to the same conclusion. Although the Smith brothers were undeniably McLaughlin-Machine enemies there was never enough evidence to charge anyone for Brad's murder. Ultimately the killing was declared an unsolved crime.

Shortly after McLaughlin first became mayor in 1927 he turned down a raise to his measly $1,500 annual salary by hinting that he expected to supplement the salary with regular bribes from gambling interests. "Don't worry about me," he said. "Leo will get his." Thereafter, Leo consistently lived beyond his apparent means during his twenty-year tenure as mayor. Among other hobbies he accumulated a stable of horses. Most notable, as explained earlier, was the Scotch and Soda pair that pulled his flashy little buggy up Central Avenue most every day of good weather. He attended horse shows in Chicago, St. Louis, Houston and New York. The 1937 National Horse Show invited him to address their convention in St. Louis.

Partly because the faultfinding propensity of his mother and sisters toward his spouses, Leo never stayed married for long. After he met his third wife, Florence, at a Houston horse show in 1931 it took only five years for the McLaughlin women to poison his attitude toward her. When she filed for divorce in 1936 she claimed he had $500,000 in assets composed mostly of cash and government bonds. She also estimated that his income averaged about $5,000 a month. While elaborating on his multiple income sources she testified that the couple would normally stop by the Southern Club where Leo would pick up an envelope stuffed with cash before the pair departed for shopping trips to Little Rock. But if Florence's accusations about Leo's wealth were accurate, her divorce settlement was modest. She received a sum of only $3,500 together with $1,800 in financial support during the pre-divorce separation.

While the community leaders realized that Judge Ledgerwood shared Leo's Machine power, Verne exercised it more subtlety. He ran his court like an assembly line on days when prostitutes and gamblers appeared to pay their fines. The repetitive fines ultimately led to deliberate attempts to disguise the names of the violators. Although state law normally declared gambling to be a misdemeanor, anyone convicted three times would be regarded to have committed a felony on the third and later incidents. As a result, Ledgerwood's clerks started using fake names. Sometimes they used automobile names: Joe Ford, Larry Plymouth, Ernest DeSoto, etc. Other times they used the names of Arkansas counties, Gus Polk, Jim Perry, J. B. Garland, and so on.

Only gambling offenders and prostitutes were allowed to use such aliases. All other lawbreakers, even for such minor offenses as disturbing the peace or public drunkenness, were booked under their real names. If they were habitual offenders they would quickly become categorized as felons, whereas the alias names available to the fine-paying gamblers perpetually kept their offenses from rising above the misdemeanor level. In short, Hot Springs had two justice standards: One for the gamblers, who provided politicians with a genteel form of bribery through a system of fake fines, and another for everyone else.[97]

Memoirist Shirley Abbott who grew up in Hot Springs during the McLaughlin era descried the atmosphere of living in a town controlled by a political machine.

> The politics were in the water, in the air, in the food ... I grew up knowing the name of every single official in the place ... If you had a car and you got a parking ticket, you would look at this parking ticket and your first thought would be "How did I get to be low enough in the pecking order to get this parking ticket in the first place?" And your second thought would be "How can I get somebody to fix this ticket so I don't have to pay it." I mean it never would occur to anybody to just go and pay the parking ticket.
>
> You knew that the town was run by a machine and you could go and see somebody...If you had a hole in the street, you went down to the courthouse and you talked to somebody. If your kid was in trouble, maybe you went down to see the mayor and said, "My boy's in trouble." And he said, "Well he's a good boy. I'll call the sheriff and see if we can't do something about that."

> And of course as the daughter of a bookie, I was also aware that there was a lot of bad stuff going on up at the top. That … a system of bribery … [and] payoffs [existed.] That there were people who were above the law … My gosh, the same guys who were patrolling the streets giving you parking tickets … were working as bouncers in the casinos at night.[98]

From his *My Life* autobiography former President Bill Clinton provides his perspective about coming of age in Hot Springs about ten years after Shirley Abbott. His family moved there from nearby Hope, Arkansas, when Bill was entering the second grade. Perhaps because he became a politician almost immediately after getting his law degree, he wrote little about the spa town's machine politics and gambling.

He did, however, write cryptically about the topic of "secrets" during this period, partly in context of his stepfather's occasionally violent alcoholism. "The question of secrets is one I've thought about a lot over the years. We all have them and I think we're entitled to them. They make our lives more interesting, and when we decide to share them, our relationships become more meaningful. Still secrets can be an awful burden … Or the allure of secrets can … make us feel we can't live without them, that we wouldn't even be who we are without them."[99]

In one of its few remarks about the town's shady reputation, Clinton's autobiography states: "The Mafia never took over gambling in Hot Springs; instead we had our own local bosses. Sometimes competing interests fought, but in my time the violence was always controlled. For example, the garages of two houses were bombed, but at the time no one was home."

He also acknowledged that Central Avenue was lined with gambling clubs and restaurants. The restaurants typically contained slot machines where he sometimes saw children playing while sitting in a parent's lap. He admitted that his mother was practically addicted to the month-long horseracing season at Oaklawn Park. Since he also mentioned that she vacationed in Las Vegas at least once, it seems logical to infer that she gambled regularly in the Hot Springs casinos.

Later Clinton enjoyed telling stories about some of the legendary visitors he met. In a 1977 charity fund raising event when he was Arkansas's Attorney General, he shot pool against Rudolf Wanderone, commonly known as Minnesota Fats. In the novel and film, *The Hustler*, which mixed imaginary and real characters, Fats was the foil to the story's fictional lead character, youthful pool hustler "Fast Eddie" Felson. Paul Newman portrayed the hustler in the 1961 film, which is set in New York. The novel, however, is set in Chicago where Fast Eddie arrived after a string of victories—with one exception—in smaller towns. The exception was in Hot Springs.

The former president remembers that Hot Springs was more racially and ethnically diverse than other Southern towns with 35,000 residents. Aside from numerous African-Americans, there were two Roman Catholic Churches and two Synagogues. Jews owned some of the best stores, including his favorite childhood toy store, Rickey's. They also built the Leo N. Levi Hospital, where Buddy Lansky visited for hydrotherapy. Clinton even became friendly with an Arab family. Their son played in the high school band with the future president and later became a Pennsylvania neurosurgeon. A large Greek Community had its own Orthodox Catholic Church that included members who owned restaurants. One of the restaurants was next to Clinton Buick, which his uncle owned and the place where his dad worked.

Finally, both Clinton and Abbott report favorably on the Hot Springs public schools. Aside from the Roman Catholics even the most prosperous Hot Springs families relied upon public education. Abbott states flatly that the high school was "ten times better than you would expect in a town that size."

Numerous teachers encouraged Clinton to become a leader, which steered him to statewide recognition in the Boy's State and summer musical band camps that drew participants from all parts of Arkansas. After Georgetown University accepted his application, Clinton worried about whether attending the school would be worth the expense, which challenged the family finances. Fortunately, the high school guidance counselor adamantly recommended that he attend, describing the expense as an investment in the future. Clinton and Abbott also write of their opposition to the racial segregation in Hot Springs, but neither mentioned any friendships with African-Americans their own age while living in the town.[100]

For seven years after his 1927 election, Mayor McLaughlin persistently tried to gain authority to renew horse racing at Oaklawn Park where it had been closed down by the state legislature in 1919, partly at the urging of the town's reform-minded citizens. Bills to reauthorize Oaklawn racing were introduced in three straight sessions of Arkansas's alternate year legislatures in

1929, 1931, and 1933. Governor Harvey Parnell vetoed the 1929 bill, which was the only one to get through both chambers of the legislature. Finally, there was a glimmer of hope when a Ledgerwood fishing buddy, Junius Futrell, became governor. Futrell told the judge that he would sign a racing bill if one made it through the legislature.

Hot Springs Skyline From Oaklawn Park | Courtesy of Richard DeSpain

Although the legislature would not meet again until 1935, Leo sprang into action. He convinced Oaklawn's St. Louis based owners to open a three-week exhibition season in March 1934. Objections from across the state immediately swamped the new governor. Some even suggested that he mobilize the National Guard to block Oaklawn's re-opening. In response, Futrell asked the state's Attorney General to provide a legal opinion regarding a governor's authority to use the National Guard for such purposes. After due consideration the attorney general replied, "I do not think that it was ever contemplated that the military forces of the state should be used to prevent the commission of misdemeanors … [when] no violence is used and there is no injury to person or property."

Leo was elated. On 1 March 5,000 fans showed up at the track's enclosed and heated grandstand. On St. Patrick's Day, 12,000 fans filed into the grandstand, including former Governor Parnell who had vetoed the 1929 bill that would have authorized racing five years earlier. On the final day of the season 15,000 spectators packed into the stands, which may have been the largest crowd to attend an Arkansas sporting event up to that date. Finally, in 1935 a bill that included an entertainment tax was enacted re-authorizing racing at Oaklawn Park. During its first year, the tax generated over $100,000, which was a respectable sum for the small, impoverished state during the depths of the Great Depression.

Oaklawn became a well-liked track. At one time it ranked fifth in national attendance despite its remoteness from the country's population centers. Its owners believed that the track's popularity partly reflected the absence of gimmick betting, such as Exactas and Trifectas. They also felt that fans approved of its strict rules against pre-race medications for the horses.[101]

In 1940 Leo became executor to the estate of Gambling Czar William S. Jacobs when Jacobs died intestate. Jacobs had never married and had no children. His estate, which included ownership interests in six nightclubs, including the Ohio, Kentucky, Southern, White Front, Belvedere and Ozark, was generally believed to be worth over half a million dollars.

Leo's performance as executor was suspicious. Although it was commonly known, for example, that Jacobs held some jewelry as collateral for certain debts owed to him by unlucky gamblers, the jewelry never appeared on any estate inventory list. Since Leo took more than the state's mandatory five years to complete the paperwork, the estate had to pay a penalty in addition to a $10,000 inheritance tax. Leo's documents listed the estate's total value at only $271,000 from which he deducted $139,000 in claims and expenses thereby leaving $132,000 for the Jacobs heirs. The amount of money that ended up in Leo's pocket is unknown.[102]

It is likely that Owney Madden began to take equity interests in some local gambling operations during the Jacobs's estate settlement period. According to Madden biographer Graham Nown, gangsters Frank Costello and Myer Lansky were silent partners in Madden's gambling businesses. Ultimately the most notable among such operations was a 1950s-era wire service for horse race bookmakers.

Although Hot Springs racing fans could place bets with bookmakers for races anywhere in the country and wait a day to inspect the newspaper results in order to learn if they held a winning ticket, the delay ruined wagering interest. Gamblers wanted to hear a race announcer describe each race in real time for two reasons. First, it added excitement to the experience. Second, they wanted to know their winnings after each race in order to help them decide how much to bet on the next race. As a practical matter, therefore, Hot Springs bookmakers needed a wire connection to tracks around the country.

In the early part of the twentieth century Western Union transported race results to clients over its telegraph lines, but after several major shareholders objected the company discontinued the service. A shadowy Chicago company filled the gap by secretly communicating the results over Western Union lines in code. The Annenberg family acquired the successor of the Chicago-based wire service in the late 1920s. Although the Annenbergs became famous for philanthropy after the sale of their publishing businesses to Rupert Murdoch in 1988, some early Annenberg newspapers had underworld connections. For example, they sometimes employed gangs to violently disrupt the circulation of competing newspapers. During the Great Depression the family's most profitable newspaper may well have been *The Daily Racing Form.*

After Moses Annenberg was convicted for income tax evasion in 1940 another Chicago company, the Continental Press, took charge of the wire service. It continued to control the market until the early 1950s when organized crime hearings sponsored by Tennessee's Senator Estes Kefauver disclosed Continental's role and essentially forced it out of business with adverse publicity. Underworld figures like Owney Madden filled the resulting vacuum for two reasons.

First, bookmakers often declined to simultaneously own race wire operations in order to avoid federal—as opposed to state—violations. Thus, Hot Springs bookies did not normally risk running their own wire services because they could not rely upon the McLaughlin Machine to protect them from federal charges. The mayor could only insulate them against local and state law enforcement.

Second, since the Kefauver Committee recommended that "The transmission of gambling information across state lines ... be regulated so as to outlaw any service devoted to ... providing information used in illegal gambling" wire operators needed to be wealthy enough to engage the expensive legal talent required to stay on the right side of evolving federal laws. Sometimes it might even be necessary to have connections to gangland members who were experienced in the variety of wicked methods that might be used to deter attention from federal authorities, including bribery, blackmail and threats.

One example involved Senator Kefauver and mobster Meyer Lansky. The hearings were among the first televised congressional inquiries and were hugely popular. They were conducted in fourteen cities and involved about six hundred witnesses. An estimated thirty million viewers watched the selective proceedings that were televised. Surveys indicated that 72% of Americans were familiar with the hearings. The TV audiences were even bigger than those for the World Series or heavyweight boxing championships. "Taking the Fifth Amendment" became common expression during the 1950-51 investigations.

Gangster Frank Costello's reputation never recovered from the damage caused by the live broadcast of his testimony. Although his lawyer persuaded the committee that TV cameras should not be permitted to focus on his client's face, the cameras instead concentrated on his nervous hands. In combination with his husky Marlon-Brando-Godfather voice, the images convinced viewers that Costello was evil. Consequently, after the hearings, rumors suggested that Costello would retire from the Mafia, much like Owney Madden had done. Since he had been a regular Hot Springs visitor for twenty-five years, speculations circulated that Costello would also move to the town, which the gangster felt compelled to publicly deny.

The Costello debacle convinced Lansky that he must somehow limit his testimony to an untelevised session. Ultimately, Lansky discovered that Kefauver had a weakness for gambling and used it to blackmail the Tennessee senator.

Central Avenue - 1957 | Courtesy of Richard DeSpain #

As a youth, Kefauver taught one year of high school mathematics in Hot Springs and may have picked up his gambling habit at that time. As an adult he sometimes visited Hot Springs during its horseracing season. Prior to Lansky's scheduled testimony the mobster met several times with Senator Kefauver behind closed doors.

Sometimes he met privately. At other times his lawyer, Moses Polakoff, accompanied him. Polakoff also counted Jack Dempsey, Lucky Luciano and other edgy figures among his clients. According to Lansky's daughter, her dad showed Kefauver a stack of the senator's gambling IOUs that the crime boss had purchased. It was enough to keep Lansky's testimony off of television. The committee did, however, interrogate him three separate times without TV cameras.

In the early 1950s fewer than 30% of American homes owned televisions and nearly all network programming originated in New York. In order to stimulate demand for set sales, appliance stores put TV's in their display windows with the screens facing the sidewalk where passers-by could watch the inquires and hear them either through the picture windows or via outdoor speakers. Much of the committee's focus on Lansky involved his South Florida and Saratoga, New York, gambling operations rather than his New York City activities. After the Kefauver hearings motivated local authorities to close his illegal facilities in Florida and Saratoga, he turned his attention to Cuba where he hoped to build the biggest legal gambling Mecca in the Western Hemisphere.

Among Hot Springs residents, Owney's Mafia connections made him the obvious choice to provide a new wire service to local bookies. By the late 1950s his Downtown Printing Company was operating one of the largest such services in the South. He received his feed from New Orleans where it originated at the Nola Printing Company, which was operated by a Frank Costello representative. From his suite in the Ritter Hotel, Owney had a panel of electrical switches that enabled him to cut off any bookie that was not up to date on his bills from The Downtown Printing Company.

The better bookies offered comfortable chairs where patrons could watch wall-mounted electric boards that displayed race results and status updates at tracks from across the country. Slot machines were also generally available. Although such facilities are common today in Las Vegas and other legal settings, they were rare luxuries in the 1950s.

The 1961 federal Wire Act finally outlawed race wires. Nonetheless, subterfuge operators continued to illegally use telephone lines, although they ran the risk of easy conviction if they got caught. Decades later Internet Service Providers were exempted from liability for the traffic carried by subscribers of their networks. Thus, offshore bookies are thriving at this writing, although sports books have replaced horse books as the more popular of the two gambling forms.[103]

The McLaughlin Machine's most troublesome problems typically happened when it failed to back a winning gubernatorial candidate. In addition to its initial failure to back Governor Bailey, the Machine failed to support Homer Adkins who was the state's governor during World War II from 1941 to 1945. Adkins was sensitive to anti-gambling interests throughout the state and announced shortly after his inauguration, "If ... local forces are not utilized to correct [gambling] violations I shall make use of such forces as are at my command to secure proper respect for the laws of the state ..."

Finally, in October 1941 the governor sent state police to Hot Springs to meet with the sheriff. Word of a possible raid leaked to the casinos, which shut down temporarily. But it was not long before horseracing bookies reopened and operated more discreetly. A month after the December 7, 1941, attack on Pearl Harbor, Hot Springs gambling was once again wide open. Therefore, Adkins cracked the whip again and continued raids through the summer of 1942. There was, after all, a World War in progress that left the public with little sympathy for gamblers who stayed home while most able-bodied men risked their lives in military service.

In late 1943 the Arkansas Supreme Court overturned the decisions of two lower courts that had prevented the state police from raiding Hot Springs gambling spots without search warrants. Shortly thereafter Adkins appointed one of the town's anti-gambling pastors, Floyd Hurst, as a justice of the peace so that Hurst could promptly issue search and seizure warrants for state police arriving from Little Rock. Ironically, Hurst's son, Q. Byrum, would later become a politically influential gambling proponent and an Owney Madden business associate. Meanwhile, the Hot Springs scenario during World War II devolved into a cat-and-mouse game that resulted in the bookies and casinos promptly returning to operation after paying only light penalties in Municipal Judge Ledgerwood's court.

Governor Adkins eventually lost interest in fighting the gamblers since the local court so often postponed the hearings or assessed minor fines. By 1944 the governor was chiefly interested in his own political ambitions, which included an unsuccessful run for the U. S. Senate. Hot Springs gamblers especially resented Adkins because he ignored the illegal activities of several bookies and backroom casinos that operated in Little Rock during the war. [104]

About the time when future President Bill Clinton was born eighty miles to the Southwest in Hope, Arkansas, Bill's future uncle, Raymond Clinton, crossed swords with Mayor McLaughlin. Bill's biological father died in an automobile accident before the future president was born. Four years later Bill's mother married Roger Clinton, who was Raymond's younger brother. Raymond owned the Hot Springs Buick dealership at a time when automobile dealerships were generally among the most prestigious and profitable businesses in small towns across America.

Raymond established a Buick dealership for Roger in Hope, Arkansas. But Roger's gambling and alcohol addiction made him a poor manager and the Hope dealership was unprofitable. As a result, Raymond probably became the future president's most constructive male family role model after Bill moved from Hope to Hot Springs when in the second grade.

Before the end of World War II, the Hot Springs airport was a crude facility with dirt runways and taxiways. During the war, however, the federal government was providing much of the money required to build airports across the country. Local communities could utilize the federal largess if they contributed only a small fraction of the amount required to build a modern airport. Although the Hot Springs municipal government declined to contribute anything, the town's chamber of commerce came up with required local funding.

Predictably, Leo wanted to orchestrate the dedication ceremonies and even wanted the new airport to be named McLaughlin Field.

Since construction was completed shortly after the end of World War II many citizens felt it would be more appropriate to name the new facility Memorial Field in honor of the town's fallen soldiers. Raymond Clinton was among those who felt that way. Five days before the airport dedication he placed an ad in one of the town's newspapers on behalf of the "Business Committee to Change Airport Name" that read in bold, black letters:

> Over 5,000 citizens demand that Leo McLaughlin call a special meeting to determine the wishes of the people in re-naming the Hot Springs municipal airport. What are you going to do Leo?

The ad initially failed to get results. Leo dedicated the field as scheduled. Less than a year later on May 30, 1947, however, it was

Arlington Hotel – 1942 | Courtesy of Ray Hanley#

renamed Memorial Airport. As shall be explained in chapter 8, the town's favorable sentiment toward returning veterans would create more trouble for Leo than merely derailing his efforts to keep his name on the airport. It would put Leo in a fight to the finish for his political future and threaten him with jail time.[105]

---

93 Orval Allbritton, *Leo and Verne*, 280-81

94 *Ibid.*, 282-83

95 *Ibid.*, 286-91

96 *Ibid.*, 363, 366-67, 374-75, 378-80

97 *Ibid.*, 384-89, 392-93, 432-34; Roy Reed, *Faubus: The Life and Times of an American Prodigal*, 316

98 Shirley Abbott, "The Bookmaker's Daughter." Interviewed by Host, *PBS Frontline*, May 28, 1996, available https://goo.gl/nD83DH [Accessed: July 10, 2017]

99 William J. Clinton, *My Life*: Large Print Edition (New York: Random House, 2004), 70

100 *Ibid.*, 38-40, 54, 102; Shirley Abbott, "The Bookmaker's Daughter." Interviewed by Host, *PBS Frontline*, May 28, 1996

101 Orval Allbritton, *Leo and Verne*, 402-07, 413

102 *Ibid.*, 437-39

103 *Ibid.*, 584; T. J. English, *Havana Nocturne* (New York: William Morrow, 2007), 77-86; Sandra Lansky, *Daughter of the King* (Philadelphia, Pa.: Weinstein Books, 2014), 14, 99-101; David Schwartz, *Cutting the Wire: Gambling Prohibition and the Internet* (Las Vegas: University of Nevada Press, 2005), 118; Graham Nown, *Arkansas Godfather*, 308, 318, 332-34, 339-40; Allan May, "The History of the Race Wire Service," *Race Wire Service*, May 1999, available https://goo.gl/3tmbQg [Accessed: July 10, 2017]; *U. S. Senate. Special Committee to Investigate Organized Crime in Interstate Commerce*, 82 Congress, First Session, Report Number 275, August 31, 1951, available https://goo.gl/tufeFu [Accessed: July 10, 2017]; W. K. Bachelder, "The Suppression of Bookie Gambling by a Denial of Telephone and Telegraph Facilities," *Journal of Criminal Law and Criminology* (V. 4, N. 2) 1949, 176-77, available https://goo.gl/shz2EE [Accessed: July 10, 2017]

104 Orval Allbritton, *Leo and Verne*, 444, 450-51; James A. Pierce, "From McMath to Rockefeller: Arkansas Governor and Illegal Gambling in Postwar Hot Springs, 1945 – 1970," Thesis for Master's Degree (University of Arkansas, 2008), 15

105 Orval Allbritton, *Leo and Verne*, 467; Roger Morris, "Partners in Power: The Clintons and Their America," Interviewed by Host, *PBS Frontline*, June 13, 1996, available https://goo.gl/PwyYQA [Accessed: July 10, 2017]; City of Hot Springs, *Airport History*, available https://goo.gl/PQdQve [Accessed: July 10, 2017]; Nancy Hendricks, "Bill Clinton Boyhood Home," *Encyclopedia of Arkansas History and Culture*, available https://goo.gl/WgK8Qp [July 10, 2017]

Chapter Seven
FAITH, INTEGRITY & CHOICE

AROUND THE TURN of the nineteenth-to-twentieth century eight elegant bathhouses were built along Central Avenue. Presently only the Buckstaff and the Quapaw still operate. Among the original eight the Fordyce survives as a combination museum and interpretive center. It also serves as the Hot Springs National Park welcome center.

Samuel Fordyce, a Northern businessman who arrived in the town in 1870 on a stretcher with instructions from his doctor to attempt a cure by bathing in the mineral-rich hot waters, would later build the eponymous bathhouse. After six months of regular treatments Fordyce regained his health and lived to the ripe age of 89 when he died in 1919. His family continued to manage the bathhouse for another 43 years until it closed in 1962. The facility had marble chambers lined with tubs and needle showers. It also included hot-wrap and cold-wrap lounges as well as a hydrotherapy room with high-pressure hoses, steam cabinets and tubs, which could pass mild electric currents through the bathers.

Attendants accompanied visitors during therapy sessions to ensure that patrons did not linger too long in the tubs or steam cabinets. They also helped patients who arrived with detailed doctor-prescribed therapy instructions, such as massages and specific exercises. Other forms of relaxation were available at the Fordyce including rooms for billiards, board games, reading, and cigars. It also had a gymnasium where prizefighters such as Rocky Marciano once trained. Ladies had their own lounge as well as a beauty parlor.[106]

Modern medical science demonstrates conclusively that thermal waters are incapable of providing anything more than a temporary palliative effect. But that was not always the common belief. In the late nineteenth century, for example, about 70% of the patients treated at Hot Springs suffered from either "rheumatism"—probably a form of arthritis—or syphilis. Since at least the 1950s doctors have characterized claims about cures from such therapies as illusions or, at best, faith healings that cannot be explained scientifically. Yet at one time an entire medical journal was devoted to such treatments. Since scientific realities became increasingly obvious after World War II, the National Park Service reported a peak of one million baths in 1946, and a steady decline thereafter. Seventeen years later in 1963, for example, the number of baths dropped to a half-million—translating to a compounding annual decline rate of about four percent.

Nonetheless, prior to the advent of antibiotics and anti-inflammatory drugs, which can legitimately treat illnesses such as arthritis and syphilis, many visitors in addition to Fordyce believed the waters had cured them. Among them was Verne Ledgerwood's grandmother, Permelia. She suffered from "rheumatism" that was especially hard to tolerate during the cold Kansas winters where she lived. Sometime during the 1870s she and her husband visited Hot Springs for three weeks. Afterward Permelia pronounced herself much rejuvenated, which astonished and delighted her family.

Another advocate was Indiana-born Carrie Abbott whose granddaughter, Shirley, authored a popular memoir about growing up in Hot Springs in the 1930s and 40s, *The Bookmaker's Daughter*. But Carrie's case proved to be more typical. Her "Rheumatiz" cure was only temporary. Shirley remembers her grandmother as an invalid who lived in the same home as Shirley and her parents.[107]

Perhaps years of approving testimony about such water-therapy healings influenced the popular religions of the Hot Springs area. Even today it is near—if not directly on—the Bible Belt Buckle. Arkansas is predominantly Christian. Its largest denomination is Southern Baptist, which requires baptisms with full body immersion. It is also believed to be America's second largest Christian denomination behind Roman Catholicism. Even more in evidence across the state, if not more numerous, are various groups of Evangelical Christians that interpret the Bible narrowly, or even literally.

One example is the Assemblies of God, which was formally organized in Hot Springs in 1914. Currently the church claims to be the world's largest Pentecostal denomination with nearly seventy million members in over two hundred countries. Pentecostal sects often interpret the Bible literally, which leads many members to believe in faith healing and glossolalia. The latter is commonly known as speaking in tongues.

Like the historical Confederate States of America, of which Arkansas was a member, the Assemblies of God is more a confederation of autonomous but loosely associated church groupings than a monolithic organization ruled from a central headquarters. Its Pentecostal foundation is only indirectly derived from the Jewish feast to celebrate the Ten Commandants every year on the fiftieth day after Moses carried them down from Mount Sinai. Instead it originates with the appearance of the Resurrected Christ to his disciples on the first Pentecost after his crucifixion. During that appearance his disciples "received the Holy Spirit." Once anyone receives the Holy Ghost, Pentecostal believers conclude they have been accepted into the body of Christ.

Fordyce Bathhouse | Library of Congress

Although some chapters do not follow the doctrine, strict Pentecostals sometimes require that members demonstrate concrete evidence of having received the Holy Spirit. The two most common types of such evidence are glossolalia and faith healing. To non-believers glossolalia is an unintelligible vocalizing of speech-like syllables. To exacting Pentecostals, however, it is a Divine language. Even if they cannot understand it themselves, they believe it is discernible to God. Practitioners believe it to be a gift from God that cannot be received without faith. Unsurprisingly, faith is also their foundation to Biblical healing.

Authority for glossolalia is derived from several New Testament excerpts, but the most common are in Versus 2-4 of the Second Chapter in the Book of Acts, which describe the first Christian Day of Pentecost:

> And suddenly there came a sound from heaven as a rushing mighty wind and it filled all the house … And there appeared unto [Jesus's disciples] cloven tongues like as of fire, and it sat upon each of them. And they were all filled with the Holy Ghost and began to speak with other tongues as the Spirit gave them utterance.

Much like glossolalia, rigorous Pentecostals believe that the power to heal physical ailments is a gift of the Holy Spirit. Non-believers cannot receive the gifts. Faith in the power of the Holy Ghost is necessary. To those without faith, both gifts are incomprehensible. Moreover, the two are often coupled based on Verses 17-18 of the Sixteenth Chapter of Mark:

> And these signs shall follow them that believe. In my name shall they cast out devils; they shall speak in new tongues; they shall take up serpents; and if they drink any deadly thing, it shall not hurt them; they shall lay hands on the sick and they shall recover.

By 1913 the Pentecostal denominations had proliferated to a point where non-credentialed evangelists were spreading erroneous doctrine that confused the believers and threatened the movement. Occasionally, for example, missionaries went overseas on missions without any language capabilities beyond English and glossolalia. The chaotic results were predictable.

As a result, in December 1913 one Pentecostal leader who published a church magazine and happened to live near Hot Springs called for a general council to meet at the resort town in April 1914. The town's gambling and other vices were on the decline at the time for two reasons. First was the town's focus on recovering from a devastating September 1913 fire. Second was the temporary ascendancy of a reform-minded local government as discussed earlier, which was gradually driving out drummers and medical quacks and forcing gambling into back street dives.

The council call was controversial because Pentecostalism was anti-denominational and some members feared any move toward centralized authority. Nonetheless, about 40% of the three hundred conventioneers that arrived were ministers and missionaries. A total of twenty states, and some foreign countries, were represented. Most representatives arrived from Southern, Great Plains, Midwestern and Mountain states.

Hot Springs residents took little note of the convention. It was easily dismissed as an obscure religious sect that was unlikely to amount to much. Nonetheless, the delegates took their work seriously and voted to organize as the General Council of the Assemblies of God. Although the sect moved its headquarters to Springfield, Missouri, the Assemblies and other evangelicals became popular religious groups around Hot Springs for the remaining era of illegal gambling as well as into the present.[108]

The contrast between the strict moral prohibitions of the popular religious orders in the Hot Springs area and the gambling, vices, and corruption that were common for so many years in the Devil's Town needs reconciliation. Few pastors of any denomination, for example, went to battle against the McLaughlin Machine, or other corrupted rulers. Much like the protruding nail that gets pounded down, those who did often wish they hadn't.

One example was Reverend C. F. J. Tate who had a home near the Oaklawn Park racetrack. When he tried to get a bill through the state legislature that would outlaw all racetracks within three miles of a school or church, town leaders vigorously opposed him and the legislators rejected it. When a 1935 bill to legitimize horse racing at Oaklawn was introduced in the legislature, the Arkansas Baptist Convention sent eight delegates under the leadership of a Hot Springs pastor to meet with the applicable House committee in an effort to block the bill. They failed.

When Reverend Claude Jones of the town's First Christian Church sensed that the local political Machine was divided over gubernatorial candidates in 1940, he led a delegation to ask Arkansas Circuit Court Judge Earl Witt to authorize a grand jury investigation into illegal gambling. Witt bluntly told Jones that previous grand juries had concluded that bookmaking as it existed under the McLaughlin Machine was preferable to earlier practices because the routine fines provided steady revenue for the city. He added that Jones would have his best chance of changing the situation by persuading the legislature to classify gambling as a felony instead of a misdemeanor. Such action would require that Jones approach local state representatives who were known to be part of the McLaughlin Machine. Jones and his colleagues had mistaken internal differences over gubernatorial preferences within the Machine as a fundamental split in the Machine over gambling.[109]

Although religious group opposition to gambling might have occasionally threatened the casinos, bookmakers, and slot machine parlors, the bathhouses probably benefitted from a spiritual culture that encouraged belief in faith healing. The testimony of witnesses like Samuel Fordyce who claimed that they had been healed by the thermal waters were likely taken more seriously by such believers. When evaluating the efficacy of the spa's hydrotherapy, resident Dr. Francis Scully, M.D., who authored a 1966 book on Hot Springs, wrote: "The mental attitude of the individual [patient] has a very decided influence on the body and its functions, much more than realized by the average person."

Whether the cures of patients who testified to the validity of the spa's hydrotherapy were miracles—or illusions—it's likely that most who got favorable results believed permanent healing was at least possible. Otherwise it is necessary to suppose that visitors—particularly those from out-of-state—planned a long and expensive trip for nothing more than a temporary benefit. Presently, for example, few visitors expect Hot Springs water to provide a lasting cure. That's why only two of the eight elegant bathhouses on Central Avenue still operate.[110]

Finally it's likely that many religious leaders acquiesced to the presumed immorality of illegal gambling, prostitution, and corrupted local government because of the income such vices provided to the community and thereby indirectly to the religious institutions. Some of the churches had even habitually accepted donations from the gambling interests.

Although the cynical wisdom that "money makes the world go 'round" had its influence, it is important to appreciate that such temptations are more powerful for the economically needy than for others. Since the end of the Civil War, Arkansas has always ranked near the bottom of states when measured by per capita income. Presently it ranks forty-eighth out of fifty, but during the illegal gambling era only Mississippi was poorer. In 1950, for example, the per capita incomes in each of Illinois, Massachusetts, and New York were more than twice as much as those in Arkansas. Similarly the average per capita personal income for all forty-eight states in 1950 was more than 75% higher than Arkansas's average.[111]

Scriptwriter Nunnally Johnson provides an enlightening analysis of a similar situation in the film, *The Man in the Gray Flannel Suit,* which is based upon Sloan Wilson's novel. When a rising young New York broadcast industry executive is tempted to endorse a dubious proposal hatched by his boss, the young executive first discusses the situation with his wife privately at home. The wife dogmatically accuses her husband of cowardice for merely even considering that he should decline to give his boss a truthful, but critical, opinion.

> *Betsy Rath:* I want you to go out and fight for something you believe in, not to turn into a cheap slippery 'yes' man.

> *Tom Rath:* Wonderful! Would you think about this for a minute or two?
>
> When a man's got plenty of security, money in the bank, and other jobs waiting for him, it's a cinch to be fearless and full of integrity. But when he's got a wife and children to support and his job is all he's got, what do you think he ought to do about it then?[112]

Collier's Weekly writer Walter Davenport tells of meeting a conflicted and dubiously-credentialed preacher on his 1931 drive from Little Rock to Hot Springs for his profile story noted earlier. On one of the many turns in the highway the Reverend Quapaw Jones had painted a warning on a rock outcrop over the road, reminding Hot Springs bound travelers that "the wages of sin are death." Davenport stopped to talk to Jones who would, at no charge, explain the everlasting dangers to your soul in the town ahead. But for a dime, he would tell you how to visit Hot Springs without getting morally contaminated. And for a quarter, or more, he would grant you general dispensation "on the ground that anyone with your generosity is equipped with a mind too high for the devil to reach."[113]

Thus, it's easy to reject questionable enticements when there are only minor consequences for turning them down. As shall be explained in chapter 10, it was precisely the election of a governor who was too wealthy to be tempted by Hot Springs bribery that brought an end to the town's illegal gambling. But for ordinary residents linked to the gambling trade the consequences of rejecting temptation could be grim. The wages of outlawing sin appeared to be poverty. Memoirist Shirley Abbott, for example, describes the penalties to her family after her bookmaking father was forced to seek other work following a temporary shutdown of the trade in the late 1940s.

Her Indiana born city-slicker dad began reading magazines such as *Progressive Farmer* and ordering books on farming. "This just may be the year for me to get out of the rackets," he announced. Reading aloud in the evenings had been a family custom for years. Presently, he started reading about the joys of farming such as raising boysenberries and strawberries. Shirley's mom grew anxious about her husband's turn of mind because she had grown up on an Arkansas farm and knew it to be a hard life.

She told him, "I married you to get off the farm and I don't have any idea of moving back to one."

"But you don't understand," he answered. "You came from an old-style farm. Your mama and daddy farmed the old the hard way. No equipment. No electricity. No running water. Outdoor toilets. Hoeing cotton. Slaughtering hogs. All due respect to your papa and mama, but they had no education, no understanding of agriculture as a science. [Our's] will be a modern farm .... We'll live off the fat of the land. Six hours' work a day, maximum, and we'll sit in our house by the side of the road and watch the world go by."

Mom replied, "I never saw a farm like that. You won't see one either. Besides you don't know one end of a cow from the other. You don't know a hen from a rooster."

In an effort to win over his daughter, Shirley's dad said they could get a horse if they owned a farm.

Shirley's mom continued, "A horse! What will we need a horse for? Do you know what it costs to keep up a saddle horse? You're not talking about a horse with two-dollars on his nose."

Nonetheless, the family sold their home in town to buy a farm. Shirley shirked as much as her dad would permit in order to avoid farm chores such a gardening and feeding the chickens. She hated farm life isolation, not to mention the snakes and the horrible number and variety of bloodthirsty insects.

Although her mother slipped tight lipped into the routine of a farmer's wife, her dad's inexperience soon became evident in the poor results, which did not reflect a lack of effort. Under a generally hot sun he plowed, set fence posts in concrete, and cleared the land. His fingernails became broken and dirty and his hands calloused. The boysenberry and strawberry plants promptly died. He laboriously planted the peach and apple orchards on the north side of a hill where they could not flourish.

Soon Shirley's dad became thin with overwork and undernourishment. Money was so scarce that a toothache, hole in a shoe sole, or a need for eyeglasses quickly evolved into tragedies. Shirley learned sadly that if she broke, wore out, or misplaced any personal possession, she would have to do without. Like the majority of rural Arkansas schools at the time, Shirley's nearest high school lacked accreditation. After she told her dad, "You might as well let me quit school as send me there" he agreed to let her attend school in town, although she would be helpless on days when the car would not start. It was a forty-five-minute drive.

Without illegal gambling the Hot Springs economy was dying. Long-term residents were moving away to find a new start. Bank deposits were declining and merchants were boarding-up their storefronts. Among the most depressing symbols to the Abbott family was the steady physical decline of their former home in town, which the new owners failed to maintain.

Fortunately for the Abbotts, illegal gambling sputtered back to life in Hot Springs after about five years of farming. Thereafter, Shirley's dad began driving every day from the farm to the town where he returned to horserace bookmaking. He mostly gave up farming and earned his living as a bookmaker for a few more years until one day when Shirley's mom drove to pick him up at the end of the day. He was standing on the sidewalk before he got into the car.

"I don't know what happened to me today," he said. "I was trying to figure the payoff on the fifth race, and I couldn't handle the numbers. I didn't know what they meant." His bookmaking days were over. He took the last job of his life in a turkey processing plant before dying at age sixty-three in 1966. He outlived Owney Madden by a year.[114]

Although the true figures may be under-reported, 1964 government records disclose that Las Vegas' legalized gambling revenues totaled $240 million. While the figures applicable to the illegal gambling in Hot Springs in 1964 are officially unknown, a *New York Times* investigative reporter estimated that that the town's three major casinos generated only about one-third as much revenue as a single major Las Vegas strip casino.[115]

Even though Madden was a murderer and had been a notorious gangster in New York, community leaders in Hot Springs generally accepted his presence. One reason is that he often generously distributed favors. In the early 1940s, for example, a group of Hot Springs kids traveled to New York for a band competition. The youngsters did not have much money but when they presented themselves at a ritzy New York nightclub they were given royal treatment including sophisticated dinners, all at no charge. Madden would sometimes write notes for Hot Springs residents travelling to New York stating, "To Whom it May Concern: [name of note carrier] is a good friend. Sincerely, Owney Madden." He ended the note with his phone number. Occasionally he'd write the notes inside the covers of his personalized and stylish cardboard matchbooks.

In another instance, Owney was platonically acquainted with a woman whose husband regularly beat her. When one of the beatings put her in the hospital, Owney visited and as he was leaving he told her, "This won't happen again." The next day several tough guys visited her husband on his construction job site and told him to never again beat his wife. The wife-beater immediately left town for several years. When he returned the couple divorced and the husband signed all marital assets over to his ex-wife.

Often Owney spent his mornings at the grill restaurant on the first floor of the Southern Club on Central Avenue at a regular table. If others were occupying the table when he arrived and looked needy or appeared to be a young honeymooning couple, he'd pay for their meals. He never rocked the boat politically, but at the end of World War II he noticed straws in the wind that might prompt him to switch his allegiance away from the McLaughlin Machine.[116]

In sum, gangsters could sometimes be generous while the religious poor might sometimes yield to the temptations of mammon. At Hot Springs, such consequences resulted from the town's contest between illusion and reality.

---

106 Robert Cross, "Back to Bathhouse Row," *Chicago Tribune*, December 15, 2002, available https://goo.gl/oyQK4j [Accessed: July 11, 2017]

107 Ray Hanley, *A Place Apart: A Pictorial History of Hot Springs, Arkansas* (Fayetteville, University of Arkansas Press, 2011), 137; Dee Brown, *The American Spa: Hot Springs, Arkansas*, 35; Orval Allbritton, *Leo and Verne*, 10; Shirley Abbott, *The Bookmaker's Daughter*, (Fayetteville: University of Arkansas Press, 2006), 26-27

108 Edith Blumhofer, *The Assemblies of God: A Popular History* (Springfield, Mo.: Radiant Books, 1985), 34-37; Francis Scully, *Hot Springs Arkansas and Hot Springs National Park* (Little Rock, Ark.: Pioneer Press, 1966), 295

109 Orval Allbritton, *Leo and Verne*, 182, 410, 441-42

110 Francis Scully, *Hot Springs Arkansas and Hot Springs National Park*, 225

111 Roy Reed, *Orval Faubus: The Life and Times of an American Prodigal*, 319; Federal Reserve Bank of St. Louis and U.S. Bureau of Economic Analysis, "State Per Capita Personal Income," available https://goo.gl/FN8Viq [Accessed July 11, 2017]

112 Darryl Zanuck, *The Man in the Gray Flannel Suit*, directed by Nunnally Johnson (Los Angeles: Twentieth Century Fox, 1956), available https://goo.gl/7b3RCW [Accessed July 11, 2017]

113 Walter Davenport, "Sin Takes a Hot Bath," *Collier's Weekly*, August 8, 1931, 10

114 Shirley Abbott, *The Bookmaker's Daughter*, 206-7, 223-27, 243-44, 270

115 Graham Nown, *Arkansas Godfather*, 283; Wallace Turner, "Hot Springs: Gamblers' Haven," *New York Times*, March 8, 1964, available https://goo.gl/dcrZzh [Accessed July 7, 2017]

116 Graham Nown, *Arkansas Godfather*, 308-09

Chapter Eight
VETERANS REVOLT

IN THE 1940S AMERICANS regarded World War II as a sacred crusade intended to free the world from powerful dictatorships that ruled contrary to the principles of democratic government. Among other sources, the Movietone Newsreels and radio programs of the era—many available presently on YouTube—provide realistic contemporary evidence of the public passion. Domestic political machines might be overthrown by voters who were urged to consider whether rigged elections and corrupted governments should be tolerated given the sacrifices American soldiers had made to free the governments of other nations. Under such circumstances local political machines might be interpreted as an insult to the memory of those who died. Perhaps most Americans instinctively shared such a viewpoint. If the feeling was not overt, it was almost certainly a latency that could be developed into a public force by articulate and politically ambitious returning veterans.

Among such ex-soldiers returning to Hot Springs in 1946 was thirty-four-year-old Marine Lieutenant-Colonel Sidney McMath. Prior to the war he earned a law degree at the University of Arkansas in 1936 where he joined the Reserve Officers Training Corps (ROTC) and served one year as president of the student body. Since America was not at war when he graduated, his only military obligation was a mere six-month duty tour. Thus in 1937 he set up a Hot Springs law practice at age twenty-five. Over the next three years he was able to earn only a modest living. He learned first-hand that influence—which he lacked—with the McLaughlin administration was often a key requirement for building a successful business or law practice in the town.[117]

After the World War II broke out in Europe he was called into active duty to train officers in the event that America was drawn in to the fighting. During the year following Japan's surprise attack on Pearl Harbor that compelled America to join the allies, he continued to supervise various training activities. Finally, in February 1943 he was assigned a combat command, which he led into an attack on the Japanese occupied Pacific island of Bougainville, near New Guinea. His performance led to a Lieutenant-Colonelcy and also won him Legion of Merit and Silver Star awards.

Soon after returning home, McMath filed to run in the Democratic primary against the McLaughlin Machine incumbent as District Attorney for Arkansas's eighteenth judicial district, which covered the adjoining Garland and Montgomery counties. Not only did he file without McLaughlin's approval, he also persuaded other veterans and allies to compete for many of the remaining Machine offices subject to election that year.

The resulting political challenge became known as The GI Revolt because "GI" is a slang synonym for a U. S. soldiers. (The term is derived from the Government Issue labels and tags commonly included on a soldier's clothing and other personal items, which the Army issued to the soldiers.) In order to smash the McLaughlin Machine the GIs would need to oust incumbent Earl Witt as judge for Arkansas's eighteenth circuit, in addition to winning the DA post that McMath targeted. Clyde Brown, a close McMath friend, agreed to challenge Witt. Even though McLaughlin was not up for re-election until the following year, the GIs knew they could fatally weaken the Machine if McMath and Brown won the eighteenth district elections.[118]

McMath's campaign decided to contrast the free government principles that Americans had recently fought a war to promote in other countries with the corrupt Machine politics in his hometown. Shortly before the July 1946 primary he gave a radio talk in which he contrasted the recent free elections in Italy with the despotic situation in Hot Springs. American GIs, he claimed, were partly responsible for Italy's new freedoms. His GI Revolt, he stated, was similarly intended to restore honest government to Hot Springs. He went so far as to suggest metaphorically that McLaughlin was a Nazi commander who merely lacked a German accent and a swastika. When describing the mayor's campaign and governance methodologies, McMath quoted Leo as allegedly saying to a former confidant, "I get things done without internal squabbling ... I [already] know how everyone votes..."[119]

Next McMath hunted down evidence of habitual voter fraud in Hot Springs. His campaign contracted with a company specializing as independent investigators to compile numerous affidavits documenting voter fraud. He quoted some of the affidavits on his radio address. One man avowed that he had voted fourteen years without ever paying a poll tax. The same man also claimed that he was many times given free transport, along with other voters, to cast their ballots multiple times with forged receipts.

A police officer that worked as a poll guard in a 1936 election affirmed that he had observed a clerk filling out multiple ballots and selecting the candidates from a list provided by incumbent judges.

Although a screen of Machine-loyal people quickly surrounded the clerk, the policeman was able to see that the clerk stuffed the fake ballots into the ballot box.

A third affidavit from a clerk that ultimately refused to cooperate with the Machine stated that the day before the election he and other clerks reported to city hall where they were given ballots together with a list of Administration-approved candidates. When he refused to cooperate, the assigned list was given to a Machine-compliant voter.

McLaughlin struck back at a GI Revolt campaign opener. Leo learned the time and place of the GI campaign's first rally from promotional leaflets dropped from an airplane. While nearly a thousand voters and their families were listening to GI candidate speeches, McLaughlin's dirty tricksters arrived at the auditorium parking lot where they spread roofing tacks. Although sympathetic to the revolt, a columnist for the state's largest newspaper, *The Arkansas Gazette*, wrote, "Mayor McLaughlin is slicker than a bucketful of greased eels … and the GIs can expect a double injection of major league trouble; in fact, they're

Governor Sid McMath | Arkansas Governors Official Portrait

going to run into more difficulties than a guy trying to light a wet cigar in a revolving door."[120]

The GIs responded with a tactic that Leo had never before encountered. Since they anticipated that Leo would give thousands of Machine-purchased poll tax receipts to anyone who would vote for Administration candidates, the GIs resolved to expose such fraud in a court of law before Leo could carry out the habitual routine. Due to Machine control over city, county, and state judges, the GIs were forced to discover a way of getting a federal court involved. They eventually concluded that the best method would be to run a candidate for a federal office, such as congressman or senator, because a federal—not state—judge would hold jurisdiction over any legal challenges in such a race. Although it was too late to get his name on the ballot, McMath ally, Patrick Mullis, agreed to run as a write-in, token candidate against incumbent Congressman W. R. Norrell.

If the GIs could get a federal judge to invalidate fake poll tax receipts the receipts would be unavailable in both the federal or local elections. Accordingly, they filed a complaint in Judge John Miller's federal district court claiming that many Hot Springs area poll tax receipts were phony. Leo immediately sensed trouble because ten years earlier, it will be recalled, McLaughlin tried to block Miller's successful run for the U. S. Congress before the latter was appointed to his present post as a federal district judge. McMath's team discovered thousands of phony tax receipts and requested that Miller throw them out in order to prevent the receipts from being exchanged for ballots on Election Day.

Three days before the trial a gunman held up two GI campaign workers who were canvassing house-to-house in search of more irregular poll tax receipts. The thief took a distinctive briefcase that contained all of the evidence the workers had collected, which included the names of some of the people providing affidavits. Fortunately, the campaigners recognized the robber, who was a deputy assessor in the McLaughlin Administration. In response, McMath and two other GI candidates visited Mayor McLaughlin personally. They successfully demanded the return of the briefcase and "diplomatically conveyed to him that if he wanted to play rough, we have some people on our side who had recent experience in that kind of activity."

Initially the GI team had difficulty making their case in Miller's court. Some witnesses contradicted earlier signed affidavits that vowed they had never paid the poll tax corresponding to the receipt in their name. It seems likely that some were pressured to change their stories because McLaughlin's men discovered their affidavits in the stolen briefcase. Nonetheless, the ex-soldiers had stronger evidence. They were, for example, able to show that two hundred receipts had been issued in numerical order to a nightclub owner who conceded that he signed personally for the receipts. He further confessed intent to exchange the receipts for ballots on Election Day. Finally, he testified that historically two-dollar bills were sometimes attached to ballots thus acquired and given to impoverished voters wanting to make a little easy money.

The GIs were also able to show similar instances of poll tax receipt abuse involving other casino owners and well-known politicos. It was harder to demonstrate a receipt-fraud connection to a McLaughlin loyal black nightclub owner who had purchased a block of about 1,500 receipts. They had been issued in a clever sequence pattern that required the breaking of a code to verify that the nightclub owner was the solitary buyer. Nonetheless, when the broken-code analysis was presented in court it was so compelling that the defense attorneys declined to challenge it. Ultimately Judge Miller invalidated about one-fourth of the questionable Garland County receipts and directed that the names on those receipts be removed from eligibility for all applicable elections.

On the date of the Democratic primary (30 July) voters witnessed stricter compliance to election procedures than had been observed in years. Both sides had deployed numerous poll watchers. Some of the veteran group supporters used home movie cameras to record voters entering and leaving the polling stations. One watcher even blocked McLaughlin as the mayor attempted to enter a polling station where he was not authorized to vote. Some of the veterans and their supporters "toured the county, like a combat patrol, their automobiles loaded with guns." McLaughlin supporters did the same. As a result, Garland County probably had its most honest election in years.[121]

It was not, however, enough to defeat Leo's Machine. Aside from McMath all other GI team members lost their elections. McMath's exception probably reflected two factors. First, the public knew him better because he was the team leader. Second, the DA office he targeted represented two counties, Garland and Montgomery, instead of one. McLaughlin had less influence in the latter.

As the ballots were counted after the polls closed the phone lines between the two counties were mysteriously kept busy thereby preventing Leo's vote counters in Garland County from knowing the ballot breakdown in Montgomery County. Without such information they were forced to guess at the number of phony ballots that Garland County would need to fabricate in order to defeat McMath. Their guess was low. Although Clyde Brown was running against Earl Witt for a judgeship that also encompassed both counties, Witt was even more popular than McLaughlin. That's probably why GI team member Brown lost even though McMath won.

Despite their best efforts to insure an honest election the ex-soldiers were unable to eradicate election fraud. Poll tax receipts that Judge Miller had cancelled, for example, were used in two African-American wards in Hot Springs that voted decisively for Machine candidates. The margins in those wards alone gave Earl Witt the victory over Clyde Brown. The GIs also claimed that they had home movies of black voters going to the polls holding distinctive pink slips distributed by Leo's Administration identifying the incumbents as the preferred candidates.

Despite the primary defeat, the veterans did not give up. McMath announced, "The fight for free government has just begun." Instead of launching a legal challenge to the primary results, his team decided to run a second time in the November general election as candidates with no official party affiliation.

Even as late as 1946 Arkansas politics remained dominated by the Democratic Party, which meant that election results were normally determined in the primary season. Even if victorious in the November election, renegade Democrats who ran against Democratic nominees were normally blackballed from any further affiliation with the Party. Such exclusion could be fatal to the careers of ambitious of young politicians, such as the GI team. Those who might covet a statewide office in the future, such as governor, would almost certainly need to win a Democratic primary to get it. Nonetheless, it will be recalled that McLaughlin himself ran as an independent when he defeated the Democratic nominee in the 1927 mayoral election.

The GI team's irregular decision to run as independents in the general election against the local Democratic Party nominees enraged McLaughlin. Reflexively he threatened to run an independent candidate stalking horse of his own against McMath, who was the solitary GI team winner in the Democratic primary. The mayor later abandoned the idea by dubiously claiming that he wanted to demonstrate loyalty to the Democratic Party, which he hoped would give him the moral high ground among the voters who were overwhelmingly registered as Democrats.[122]

Partly because the Democratic Party dominated the state, a wrinkle in the poll tax regulations inadvertently gave the GIs a winning chance in the November general election. Specifically, access to a ballot for a primary election required a poll tax receipt that had been purchased a year earlier whereas voters in a general election were permitted to pay their poll taxes as late as four weeks before Election Day. As a result, the GIs hurriedly launched a massive poll tax drive. They reactivated telephone groups and canvassed neighborhoods to get people registered and pay their poll tax.

Although McMath was the only GI winner in the primary, his victory gave previously disillusioned voters hope that they might be able to retire the McLaughlin Machine at the polls in the general election. Before McMath's win many had simply lost faith that such a thing could happen until Leo decided to quit on his own. As a result, the GI candidates beat all of the incumbents in the November election. By any measure, it was an extraordinary reversal.[123]

The GI Revolt was mostly about restoring honest elections, which it accomplished by exposing and eliminating the poll tax frauds. McMath himself explained the evil he opposed was "not only a matter of flagrant corruption in high places. It was a matter of the systematic, calculated destruction of democracy itself ... This community of once-free citizens had lost its right to vote—the cornerstone upon which all our freedoms rest."

It is chiefly by legend that the revolt is remembered as reaction against illegal gambling *per se*, instead of a more basic rebellion in favor of free elections. In fact, some GI candidates did not even oppose gambling. For example, Clyde Brown's father-in-law formerly owned one of the town's casinos. Q. Byrum Hurst, who ran for county judge, openly favored gambling because it boosted the local economy. Aside from later winning a seat in the state Senate, he also became a legal counsel for Owney Madden who may have returned the favor by falsely saving his lawyer from a tax evasion conviction years later. Specifically, Madden testified that he loaned Hurst money that the IRS had imputed to Hurst as unreported income. During the savings-and-loan scandals of the 1970s Hurst finally served jail time for misuse of bank funds. Lastly, after becoming tax collector during the GI Revolt, Ray Owen served six terms before he was ironically sentenced to prison for poll tax fraud.

Although the Revolt did not exterminate gambling, most of the wagering activities temporarily shut down. It was the time interval when Shirley Abbott's dad moved the family out of town and purchased the unprofitable farm. Even though some of the gambling clubs would start again in a year or so, their operations were secretive and irregular. In her study of the GI Revolt, Patsy Ramsey writes, "... The only gambling in the town in the late 1940s was hidden. One of the most prominent casino operators of the 1950s referred to the gambling of 1947-1950 as 'sneak gambling' in which people surreptitiously placed bets and played the horses in garages and back rooms. The casinos had closed though 'people knew where to find [gambling] if they wanted it.'" The post-1950 renewal corresponds to the time the Abbott family moved back into town and Shirley's dad renewed his bookmaking business. [124]

McMath moved into the DA office in January 1947. Two months later a grand jury charged Mayor McLaughlin with fifteen counts of bribery and malfeasance. One charge was for misappropriating public funds to pay brother George's salary at the police department where George did not seem to have any official duties. Since he was forced to admit that he allowed illegal gambling in the city, Leo announced that he would not seek re-election after twenty years in office. His successor, who defeated a token opponent by a landslide, was a GI and partner in the in the Clinton Buick dealership. An entire new slate of aldermen was also elected. Realizing that the McLaughlin regime was finished and feeling fortunate to have avoided indictments, Judges Earl Witt and Verne Ledgerwood retired to private law practice.

Perhaps because McLaughlin's lawyers got his trial venue switched to Montgomery County, where the dethroned potentate had fewer enemies, he won acquittal on the malfeasance charges that centered on his brother George's controversial employment status on the city's payroll.

Shirley Abbott, however, remembers that Judge Witt volunteered another explanation for the Montgomery County verdict in a private conversation with the girl and her mother. She quoted him as saying, "I was personally acquainted with many of the trial jurors. They were my friends ... [and] my father's friends. I'd known most of them since boyhood. You'd be surprised what a little money can do." Abbott's memoir explains, "Once the jury was chosen, [Judge Witt] sent some fellows to each farm on a cattle-buying expedition. They had offered surprising prices two or three times above the market, and cash on the barrelhead. No promises were extracted and no contracts signed. But the farmers knew where the money was coming from."

In truth, however, the malfeasance case against Leo was weak. The defense was able to demonstrate that George showed up daily at the municipal court although nobody could explain what he did other than merely be present. The mayor maintained that he hired his brother as an undercover agent to keep track of gamblers and suspicious characters that visited the city. Finally, the presiding judge instructed the jurors that they could not convict a man—meaning George—for failing to earn his pay but only for being fraudulently paid. A year later the bribery charges against Leo resulted in a hung jury and a mistrial, which prompted McMath to drop all charges.

McMath did, however, win a conviction against a lower-ranking McLaughlin Machine member. Specifically, city attorney Jay

Rowland was convicted of bribery in a number of gambling cases. Six former operators of gambling facilities testified that they made payments to the city for the privilege of operating with minimal interference from law enforcement. Typically, each paid $50 monthly to Rowland, which he delivered to Leo's secretary. After law officers raided one of the casinos, Rowland represented the owner in court for a fee of 50% of the cash seized. A city clerk testified that local gamblers paid an aggregate of about $61,000 in monthly bribes to gain immunity during 1945 and 1946. Typically, each facility paid $130 monthly with $100 going to the city and $25 to Rowland. The recipient of the final $5 was never disclosed. Upon conviction Rowland was fined $750 and sentenced to a year in prison.

During the same conversation in which Judge Witt explained to Shirley Abbott and her mother how he thought the Montgomery County jurors were indirectly bribed to favor McLaughlin, the girl asked about "poor Mr. Rowland." Witt explained that McMath's opponents had to allow the new DA at least a partial victory. Given his many allegations during the campaign against the McLaughlin Machine, McMath could not let the Administration escape without injury. Rowland, therefore, was selected to walk the plank. Witt concluded, "Things will get back to normal. The horse books will be running again in six months. This is only a flash in the pan." But Witt would not live to see it because he died of throat cancer shortly after making his valid prediction.

Although officially a free man, Leo had lost nearly all influence. He, Verne Ledgerwood and Owney Madden later failed when they tried to get a gambling-friendly chairman appointed to the Garland County Central Democratic Committee. When he died in 1958 his home and grave were vandalized, apparently by gullible treasure hunters who suspected that the sites contained a secret money cache remaining from the wealth Leo was rumored to have stashed away during his years as mayor.[125]

McMath later claimed to have had only a single direct encounter with Owney Madden, which predictably came shortly after the former assumed his authority as district attorney. About ten-thirty one evening Owney phoned him at his home and asked for a private meeting. McMath suggested that they wait until the next day but Madden said the matter required immediate attention. Since McMath was reluctant to invite the ex-gangster into his home he suggested that they meet at the top of Cedar Hill Road, which he could reach conveniently by walking.

When McMath arrived he saw a parked car with only the light of a glowing cigarette on the driver's side. As he approached the car the driver turned on the lights. McMath saw that Owney was in the passenger seat, but also observed two men in the back seats wearing fedora hats. They looked like gangsters straight out of Hollywood central casting.

McMath asked Madden to explain the urgency. Owney said it involved a trial scheduled for two New Yorkers accused of robbing a Hot Springs jewelry store. He indicated that if the charges were dropped he would insure that the pair left town never to return. Rather than inviting a conflict, McMath said evenly that he would need to ponder the situation, ended the meeting and walked home. As he walked away he listened anxiously to hear the car's motor start-up, but he was too far away to hear it when it did. Meanwhile the hair on the back of his neck stood up.

The new DA prosecuted the two New Yorkers and a judge sent them to prison. Upon release the two ex-convicts visited Madden for a loan to get out of town. Owney's money enabled them to return to New York, while their Arkansas prison experience was enough keep them out of the state ever after.[126]

Although McMath objected to illegal gambling he was chiefly interested in winning higher state offices. He appreciated how men like Thomas Dewey and Earl Warren had leveraged their success as prosecutors to become governors of New York and California, respectively. The GI Revolt gave McMath similar publicity that might enable him to become a youthful Arkansas governor with potential national opportunities ahead. Detractors concluded that such ambition left him only secondarily interested in Hot Springs. Thus, only about a year after he became DA, some Hot Springs leaders, including at least two GI Revolt colleagues, began to agitate for the return of gaming. In January 1948 a Business Man's Party organized to "elect candidates who will serve Hot Springs rather than themselves," which was a swipe at McMath's ambitions.

In fact, McMath was elected governor later that same year. He first won a closely contested runoff election as one of the two leaders in the Democratic primary. Since that enabled him to retain his identity as a Democrat, he easily won the general election against token Republican opposition.

At least two successful GI Revolt candidates, County Judge Byrum Hurst and Tax Collector Ray Owen, admitted their sympathies with the Business Man's Party. When later asked whether some of the GIs had abandoned their original idealism Hurst answered, "Yes, some of us did. The people demanded it."

Historian Patsy Ramsey concludes, "The people of Garland County had voted to clean up local politics, but many among them supported—perhaps even depended upon—the illegal gambling industry, which could hardly exist if every politician did his duty honestly and well."

Two years after McMath became governor in 1949 conspicuous gambling returned to Hot Springs when Owney Madden's favorite casino, the Southern Club, reopened. The rigid "licensing" structure of the McLaughlin era gave way in the 1950s to an *ad hoc* form of individually negotiated bribes. Other spots, such as the Belvedere and Ohio Clubs, were back in business under similarly modified bribery arrangements. By 1953 an article in the *Chicago Tribune* described Hot Springs gambling simply as "wide open."[127]

---

117 Jim Lester, *A Man For Arkansas*, 15

118 *Ibid.*, 23; C. Fred Williams, "Sid McMath," *The Encyclopedia of Arkansas History and Culture*. April 13, 2016, available https://goo.gl/KAzFQi [Accessed July 11, 2017]

119 James Pierce, "From McMath to Rockefeller: Arkansas Governors and Illegal Gambling in Postwar Hot Springs, 1945-1970," Thesis for Master's Degree (University of Arkansas, 2008), 21

120 *Ibid.*, 24; Jim Lester, *A Man For Arkansas*, 26

121 Patsy Ramsey, "A Place at the Table: Hot Spring and the GI Revolt," *Arkansas Historical Quarterly*, V. 59, N. 4 (Winter, 2000), 416-417; Sidney S. McMath, *Promises Kept* (Fayetteville: University of Arkansas Press, 2003), 175; Jim Lester, *A Man For Arkansas*, 26-9; Graham Nown, *Arkansas Godfather*, 314

122 Patsy Ramsey, "A Place at the Table: Hot Springs and the GI Revolt," 419

123 Sidney S. McMath, *Promises Kept,* 173-74

124 Patsy Ramsey, "A Place at the Table: Hot Spring and the GI Revolt," 426

125 Shirley Abbott, *The Bookmaker's Daughter,* 215-16; Jim Lester, *A Man For Arkansas,* 31-33; James Pierce, "From McMath to Rockefeller: Arkansas Governors and Illegal Gambling in Postwar Hot Springs, 1945-1970," 27; Patsy Ramsey, "A Place at the Table: Hot Springs and the GI Revolt," 421, 423-24, 426-27

126 Sidney McMath, *Promises Kept,* 183-84

127 Patsy Ramsey, "A Place at the Table: Hot Springs and the GI Revolt," 428; James Pierce, "From McMath to Rockefeller: Arkansas Governors and Illegal Gambling in Postwar Hot Springs, 1945-1970," 32

Chapter Nine
RETURN TO NORMALCY

DESPITE HIS YOUTH, McMath lasted only two terms—four years—as governor for two reasons. First, the state's dominant electric utility company, Arkansas Power & Light (AP&L) turned out to be a political enemy. Second, he became tangled up in corruption charges when fulfilling promises to improve the state's highways.

Until his family arrived in Hot Springs in a horse-drawn wagon when he was ten years old, McMath lived in rural homes without electricity. During the next twenty-five years, he grew frustrated with the slow pace at which AP&L electrified the mostly rustic state. Consequently, as governor he promoted rural electric cooperatives, which AP&L viewed as interlopers.

Since Arkansas highways were among the worst in America, McMath significantly increased spending to improve them. With AP&L working behind the scenes, three grand juries investigated accusations of payoffs connected with his highway construction spending. Although none touched McMath personally, the third grand jury issued three indictments against men linked to the governor on charges of shakedowns of contractors for campaign contributions. Nobody was convicted, but McMath's reputation was irreparably damaged and he lost reelection for a third term in 1952. AP&L actively supported his opponent.

Partly due to such distractions, McMath gave little attention to Hot Springs gambling during his time as governor and only ordered a few small raids. Since he remained ambitious for higher office he deliberately tried to distance himself from gambling and other controversies involving Garland County. In 1954 he ran unsuccessfully against John McClellan for U. S. Senator. Predictably, AP&L supported McClellan who would later lead a Senate committee investigating Mafia influence in labor unions and major corporations. A youthful Robert F. Kennedy would serve as the committee's chief legal counsel.[128]

Meanwhile Las Vegas had transformed into the nation's gambling hub for two reasons. First, unlike in other states gambling was legal throughout Nevada. Second, Mafia financiers invested large sums to develop first-rate casinos in Las Vegas that could provide a complete vacation experience as opposed to merely gambling.

Nevada legalized gambling in 1931 when less than 100,000 people lived in the state and its population density was about one person per square mile. Legalized gaming was one of several measures the legislature adopted to stimulate the state's economy. Another was legalized prostitution on a local option basis. The state also gradually liberalized divorce laws until a petitioner need only have been a Nevada resident for six weeks before qualifying.

Nevadans paid almost no taxes and the state permitted them to incorporate most any kind of business. Shippers of goods into California, for example, sometimes inventoried merchandise in Nevada in order to avoid California warehouse taxes. In short, the state provided a legal platform that was ripe for exploitation by dubious business operators who wanted to offer gambling in a locale that would not be too distant from the population centers in adjacent California.

Despite being little more than a railroad whistle stop as late as the mid-1940s, Las Vegas was the state's most promising candidate to convert into a gambling destination resort. First, it was close to the burgeoning population of Southern California. Second, completion of the Hoover Dam during the Great Depression gave the tiny town a nearly inexhaustible supply of water and cheap electricity. The latter was famously used to power eye-catching neon signage as well as the cooling air conditioners. The latter were essential to human comfort in the otherwise often hot desert where real estate was cheap.

Since Bugsy Siegel began visiting Los Angeles from New York in the early 1930s and moved there near the end of the decade, he appreciated that nearby Las Vegas had the potential to become a national gambling center. After World War II he convinced Mafia leaders to finance construction of the Flamingo Hotel and Casino, which was the prototype for the city's present glitzy casinos. He also pioneered the use of Hollywood performers in floor shows to augment the entertainment experience of a Las Vegas vacation.

Unfortunately, the Flamingo's opening on the day after Christmas in 1946 flopped, partly because construction had not been properly completed. The resort had to be closed for an additional three months to finish the job. More consequentially, construction cost overruns convinced his financiers that Bugsy and his girlfriend, Virginia Hill, were keeping some of the construction money for themselves.

As a result, a Mafia assassin murdered Bugsy in the late spring of 1947. Less than half an hour after Bugsy was killed, new managers arrived to take charge of the Flamingo. Bugsy's murder made it almost impossible for Nevada legal authorities to doubt the sinister characteristics of the Flamingo's new owners. Much like in Hot Springs, however, the economic potential of well-financed gambling operations led them to look the other way.[129]

By the mid-1950s six major hotel-casinos had been added near the Flamingo on the Las Vegas Strip, which was then a stretch of Las Vegas Boulevard south of the town. Thereafter, casino growth in Las Vegas came to a temporary halt because of the competitive impact of a newer gambling hub in Havana, Cuba. The Nevada Gaming Commission retaliated by ruling that owners of casinos in Cuba could no longer be permitted to own gambling facilities in Las Vegas.

Havana emerged as a gambling center after the Kefauver Hearings forced Myer Lansky's illegal operations in Florida and Saratoga, New York to shut down. The Mafia originally tried to transform Havana into a gaming destination shortly after the end of World War II but the effort was abortive. After his 1946 deportation from America to Italy, Lucky Luciano transferred to Cuba in October of the same year where he intended to manage the American Mafia from Havana. He even hoped that if he bided his time for a few years he could pull enough strings to be readmitted to the United States.

President Truman would not have it. He told Cuban leaders that their country would not be permitted to import crucial American pharmaceuticals if it failed to kick-out Luciano. When the Cuban government gave in, Lansky became the chief Mafioso in Cuba, and probably then ranked as America's top gangster. But the existing Cuban administration was wary of creating the appearance of cooperating with the Mafia given Truman's hostility toward Luciano's temporary stay. In exchange for bribes they increasingly struck deals with various grifters who introduced new types of crooked games that left tourists and other gamblers with no chance of winning. As the city's scandalous reputation spread, high rollers lost interest in Havana vacations.

Cuban Dictator Batista | Library of Congress

Matters changed after Fulgencio Batista's military coup took control of Cuba in 1952. Batista decided to form an alliance with the Mafia in order to promote unrigged gambling in the island nation. Like the Nevada politicians he reasoned that licensed gaming would benefit the local economy. He also intended to divert some of the cash flowing through the casinos, slots, lotteries and other types of gaming into his own bank account. As a precaution that his own regime might collapse someday, Batista regularly sent couriers to Switzerland where much of his wealth was safely deposited beyond the reach of any non-Swiss taxing authority.

When Batista promptly invited Lansky to become Cuba's gambling Czar, the mobster eagerly accepted. Thereafter, Havana remained a gambling paradise until Fidel Castro's revolutionaries overthrew Batista's government at the end of 1958. Castro's followers immediately ransacked the casinos and vengefully wrecked the slot machines in a manner similar to the destruction of the Versailles Palace during the French Revolution, or the looting of the Winter Palace during the Russian Revolution.[130]

As a result, Las Vegas and Havana eclipsed Hot Springs gambling by the mid-1950s. Since Arkansas gambling remained illegal it was vulnerable to sporadic interference from the law depending upon the occupants of key local and state political offices. Nonetheless, as explained earlier, local government forbearance steadily increased after 1950 as bribery restarted, first informally and later systematically. In 1958 Hot Springs replaced the informal revenue-raising arrangement of repetitive fines with an ordinance taxing casinos operations. For next nine years the city disregarded court rulings that the tax was illegal and could not be collected. Additionally, during the first four years of the decade governors McMath and Francis Cherry did little to disrupt Hot Springs gambling.

The next governor, Orval Faubus, would hold the office for twelve years after first elected in 1954, although nobody could have initially predicted such a lengthy tenure. Hot Springs gaming played a role in Faubus' first win on election night when Leo McLaughlin phoned Faubus to report that Garland County tally-counters were submitting fraudulent returns in favor of his opponent. Faubus immediately contacted Hot Springs officials to suggest that, should he win the election, he would strictly enforce the state's anti-gambling laws if he suspected the returns from Garland County were fraudulent. The guys on the other end of the phone took his hint.[131]

Faubus' long period as governor mostly reflected the popularity he gained after ordering the state's National Guard to block racial integration at Little Rock's Central High School in September 1957. Even though he backed down that same month when President Eisenhower replaced the Guard with a thousand 101st Airborne Division soldiers, many voters in Arkansas, and elsewhere, felt that federally mandated school integration violated the Tenth Amendment principle of state's rights. Nonetheless, the federal soldiers were directed to enforce integration.

Suddenly the obscure governor was thrust on the national stage. Although condemned by most leaders outside the South, he received 250,000 mainly supportive letters from all over the country. Since Central High's political earthquake and its lingering aftershocks dominated public attention, Arkansas' illegal gambling faded into the political background. Consequently, until federal pressure materialized in the early 1960s, Faubus told Hot Springs leaders that he considered illegal gaming to be a local affair. He would not interfere unless asked to by the applicable community. As in the McLaughlin era, city authorities set up a system of fines in lieu of taxes. Annual crap table fines were $500 while those on blackjack tables and slot machines were proportionally less.

Since Hot Springs wagering was drawing less public attention some of the town's leaders felt the time was ripe to raise the gaming profile by building facilities that could compare favorably with the increasingly popular Las Vegas casinos and night clubs. One such leader was Harry Hastings, Sr., who was an occasional Faubus hunting companion and one of the best amateur golfers in Hot Springs and Little Rock, where he later moved.

Although Hastings served jail time during Prohibition, two years after it ended he founded the state's largest liquor distributorship in 1935. Its successor businesses presently remain operating and are family owned. They have 200,000 square feet of warehouse and office space and employ 175 people including fourth generation Hastings family members. During World War II Hastings, Sr., served in the Army Air Corps and later flew an airplane for McMath when the latter campaigned for governor.

Along with Owney Madden, Hastings became a silent financial partner to Dane Harris who built the Vapors Club, which was the most elegant Hot Springs casino when it opened in 1959. At the time, Harris was also an owner in the Belvedere and Tower Clubs. Hastings was also rumored to be the bagman for payments to Governor Faubus, but the speculation has never been proven.

Like at the Las Vegas clubs The Vapors brought well-known entertainers to Hot Springs. Examples include Mickey Rooney, Edgar Bergen, Patti Page, Vic Damone, Les Paul, Phyllis Diller, Rosemary Clooney, Liberace, Jane Russell, the Andrews Sisters, the Smothers Brothers, the McGuire Sisters, and Tony Bennett. Performers provided two floor shows nightly. Bennett first sang his signature "I Left My Heart in San Francisco" in a private rehearsal at the club. The only audience member was a bartender setting up for the night who told Damone's musical accompanist, "If you guys record that song, I'll buy the first copy."

The Vapors had a coffee shop, big lobby, dance floor, and a theater restaurant with tiered seating and a retractable stage large enough for an orchestra. One room, the Monte Carlo, could be configured for meetings, luncheons, and events. Its swank casino opened after dinner.

The advent of classy facilities like The Vapors, combined with the governor's non-interference policy, enabled Hot Springs gaming to reach its peak during the Faubus years. Although McLaughlin, Ledgerwood, and Witt no longer held offices, Mayor Dan Wolf, Municipal Judge Earl Mazander, and Circuit Court Judge Plummer Dobbs operated in a manner similar to the McLaughlin Machine, at least in terms of illegal gambling. When asked, Dobbs publicly remarked that he was unaware of any wagering at local clubs even though he had been repeatedly seen patronizing such places. His bogus public denials would continue until a bomb wrecked the porch of his home one morning in 1963.[132]

A 1957 incident in upstate New York prompted the U. S. Senate to conduct new Mafia investigations to follow those of Kefauver about six years earlier. Specifically, in November an estimated one hundred Mafiosi attended a summit near Apalachin to discuss various businesses such as narcotics trafficking, gambling, and loan sharking.

Local police became suspicious when expensive cars with out-of-state license tags started arriving in the sleepy town. About sixty mobsters were arrested. More than one third were employed by unions or worked in labor relations. Arkansas Senator John L. McClellan chaired the new Select Committee on Improper Actives in Labor and Management and Robert F. Kennedy was the

Committee's chief counsel. Despite the obscure title, the committee was principally investigating Mob activities, especially racketeering involving labor unions and large companies. Ultimately the hearings sparked the 1959 Landrum-Griffin Act, which regulated union elections.

Although the Select Committee released its final report in 1960, McClellan started a separate three-year investigation through the Senate's Permanent Investigations Subcommittee in 1963. It was during these proceedings that Joseph Valachi's sensational testimony prompted author Peter Maas to write his Mafia exposé, *The Valachi Papers.*

Politicians outside Arkansas increasingly resented McClellan's hearings because the interrogations disclosed Mob activity in their states while ignoring Hot Springs where illegal gambling was common and Mob influence was suspected. Columnist Lee Mortimer of the *New York Daily Mirror* wrote: "I'm just wondering why Senator McClellan of Arkansas never mentions Hot Springs, with its open gambling, slot machines and easy gals to entertain visiting Mafia and labor union big shots from all over the country?" McClellan was not only from Arkansas, but his hometown was less than one hundred miles from Hot Springs. Moreover, Garland County provided generous donations to his political campaigns. To appease critics, in September 1961 McClellan subpoenaed Owney Madden and one of his underlings. Both revealed nothing by taking the Fifth Amendment.[133]

When Robert Kennedy became Attorney General that same year he drew on his experience with the Select Committee to set two priorities. First was to break the backbone of organized crime.

Second was to end its influence with labor unions. He pressured J. Edgar Hoover's FBI, which had been focusing on mostly imaginary Communist plots, to get results against the Mob. Since the FBI did not have authority to enforce the laws of individual states Hoover generally kept the Bureau out of Hot Springs. Two exceptions were incidents like the Kansas City massacre, which originated with the capture of Jelly Nash at a Central Avenue pool hall, and the campaign to capture Alvin "Ray" Karpis when he was Public Enemy Number One and using Hot Springs as a sanctuary town. Pressured by Kennedy, however, the FBI sent investigators to Hot Springs in 1961 to explore the depths of corruption and search for federal violations.[134]

Later that year the federal Justice Department tried to move against the Southern Club. The attempt flopped because a federal grand jury failed, by a solitary vote, to indict. The case was presented as a violation of a new federal law that outlawed interstate commerce for the purpose of furthering the operation of gambling facilities in states where such wagering was illegal. Among the evidence against the Southern Club was a stack of checks from banks domiciled in other states that were written by patrons of the club. Some witnesses even testified that their out-of-state checks were used specifically for buying gambling chips. Such testimony was designed to demonstrate that money transferred via interstate commerce was used in the Club's gaming activities, which were undeniably illegal in Arkansas.

Fortunately for the Hot Springs gambling interests, the judge instructed the grand jury that their authority to indict required evidence that the profits—not merely the money used to purchase chips—moved through interstate commerce. The restrictive qualification probably explains why the jury failed to indict the Southern Club. Thereafter, Hot Springs gaming operators tried to stay clear of activities that might directly link their illegal businesses with interstate commerce. They would instead try to hide behind the fiction that they were uninvolved in interstate commerce even though most of their customers were visitors from other states. They would, for example, advertise their floor shows with radio spots, but the ads never mentioned gambling.[135]

Two of Robert Kennedy's assistants returned to Hot Springs in 1964. After visiting the casinos one night they announced at a press conference the following morning that they would take their evidence of illegal gambling to a new grand jury. Since Faubus had been warned in advance, his defensive political machinery was already in motion. Arkansas's House of Representatives had hurriedly passed a fig leaf resolution urging that Hot Springs officials enforce the state's anti-gambling laws. Faubus ostentatiously, but insincerely, endorsed it. On March 28, 1964 he went even further when newspaper headlines read, "Faubus Orders Doors of Casinos Closed; Police Will Comply." It was the first major disruption of Hot Springs gaming since 1947 when Mayor Leo McLaughlin resigned.

Hot Springs officials predicted that nine hundred workers would lose their jobs and the local economy would drop by $50 million if the casinos were forced to shut down. In response, the officials threw a Hail Mary in the form of an attempted amendment to the state constitution that would permit gaming in Garland County. If passed, the amendment would allow gambling to be legalized in the county by local referendum. It further stipulated that there could be no more than one casino for every 7,000 residents and required that casino owners be Arkansas residents who had lived in the state for at least twenty years. By June they gathered 75,000 signatures, which was more than twice as many as needed to put the amendment on the November 1964 ballot.

The November general election was also important to Hot Springs and Arkansas for a second reason. Specifically, it was the first time since Reconstruction that a Republican had a realistic chance of becoming governor. One of oil-tycoon John D. Rockefeller's grandsons, Winthrop, ran as the GOP's candidate. He had enough money and prestige to be a serious challenger. Partly due to a World War II friendship with a Little Rock soldier while the two served in the Pacific, Rockefeller moved to Arkansas in 1953. He purchased a ranch on Petit Jean Mountain about 65 miles west of Little Rock. In 1955, Faubus appointed him chairman of a state commission organized to attract new industry to Arkansas. Rockefeller also initiated a number of philanthropies and projects. He financed the construction of medical clinics in some of the state's poorest counties and made annual gifts to the state's colleges and universities.[136]

One reason that Rockefeller hoped to win in a contest with the gambling-compliant Faubus in 1964 was linked to the internecine violence between Hot Springs gaming rivals that materialized in 1963. Conceptually, the clash was a miniature version of Chicago's Capone-Moran War of the 1920s that culminated in the 1929 St. Valentine Day Massacre. In January 1963 a bomb exploded at The Vapors. Eleven people in a roulette training class were injured, although none seriously. The blast blew a hole in the roof and shattered the lobby, causing $125,000 in damages. Another bomb later exploded at the home of Dane Harris who, as noted, was the principal owner of The Vapors. Later that same month a third bomb wrecked the porch of Circuit Judge Plummer Dobbs's home. Finally, three months after the Dobbs blast a fourth bomb exploded in the unoccupied car of Prosecuting Attorney David Whittington.

Although the crimes were never solved, Harris believed the explosions were the work of two smaller casino operators who felt local politicians gave The Vapors preferential immunity from law enforcement. There was not, however, enough evidence to charge the men that Harris suspected. Since there were no indictments, much less convictions, many Arkansans speculated that outside Mafia groups were trying to move in.

Despite running as an anti-gambling candidate, Rockefeller equivocated during a May 1964 interview on NBC's "Meet the Press." When asked about his opinion on legalizing casino gambling in Arkansas he answered:

"I am very much in favor of putting this question to the people. This has been a political football for generations."

Seeking clarification, interviewer Lawrence Spivak asked, "But your position, Mr. Rockefeller; are you for or against legalized gambling in Arkansas?"

"I am for letting the people of the state take the position they want and speak for themselves."

A puzzled Spivak persisted, "You don't have an opinion about it?"

Finally, the candidate replied, "Yes. I have seen nothing about legalized gambling that I think is good. I think it is morally wrong."[137]

Faubus responded to the Rockefeller challenge predictably and effectively. Since the native Arkansan grew up in the Ozark hills when kerosene and coal oil lanterns provided households with light, he sensed an opportunity for a populist attack on Winthrop's Rockefeller ancestors.

"When I was a boy," Faubus told audiences, "I remember how hard it was [when] old man John D. Rockefeller raised the price of coal oil a penny. It was my job to stick a sweet potato on the spout of the jug and keep it from spilling out, because at the prices the Rockefellers charged, we couldn't afford to spill a drop."

A widely circulated Faubus campaign handbill contained a photograph of Rockefeller with a trim haircut. The circular explained, "Winthrop Rockefeller, the millionaire, still has to go back to New York for his haircuts." An unidentified writer illegibly signed the printed remark and added by way of context, "My yearly income is roughly $6,000. I drive a $2,500 car sixteen miles to my barber for haircuts."

The governor also charged that Rockefeller owned a casino in Puerto Rico. The false accusation apparently originated from the fact that Winthrop's brother, Laurence, owned Puerto Rican properties including a hotel that contained a casino.

Faubus's skilled Arkansas-styled campaigning was too much for Rockefeller even though the governor's repeated attempts to advertise his impoverished rural background occasionally didn't work. One humorous incident in the flat lands of south Arkansas merits sharing. As he and his team were driving to a campaign stop, they passed a lone African-American hauling three big logs to a sawmill in a mule-drawn wagon. Since several reporters accompanied the governor's group, Faubus ordered the caravan to stop so that he could offer to relieve the black teamster for a while.

Soon after the governor started the mules at a trot the wagon began to careen uncontrollably down a hill. Faubus and everyone else became frightened. Eventually, he got the mules stopped. After stepping down from the wagon he remarked that the vehicle did not have any brakes. "I noticed that when I got on it, but back where I lived in the hills all wagons had to have brakes or they wouldn't have [survived.]"

To create the appearance of honoring his pledge to shut down illegal gambling, Faubus authorized a raid two weeks before the general election. The police targeted a small bar that had only three slot machines. But that was excuse enough for Faubus to hold a press conference announcing that he "kept his word" to close illegal gambling. When the charges against the bar owner were later dismissed, Faubus proclaimed he was "flabbergasted."

In the end, Rockefeller made a good showing. He got more than twice as many votes as any previous Republican. He finished with about 44% of the general election tally, which was also one of the highest general election turnouts in memory. Moreover, the amendment that would have authorized Garland County to hold a referendum to legalize gambling locally was soundly defeated. It carried only three of seventy-five counties and lost statewide by a two-to-one margin.[138]

Following Faubus's 1964 reelection, Hot Springs nightclubs and casinos were reorganized as private clubs. Each visitor was required to have a membership before entering. But guests at local hotels discovered that free memberships were included as a standard amenity. As private clubs, their lawyers argued, the casinos were entitled to the same legal protections as privately-owned homes. Thus, law enforcement raids would require the raiders to get search warrants from a judge located in the same county as the clubs.

The excuse provided by the private club legal fig leaf enabled the governor to revert to form and proclaim that he was unaware of any illegal gambling in Garland County. This time, however, someone challenged the insincere mantra. Specifically, Republicans officially accused Faubus of ignoring the mandate, implied by the defeat of the gaming amendment, to stop illegal wagering.

Secret informants convinced the chief of the state police that Hot Springs casinos were back in business by the end of February 1965, less than four months after Faubus was reelected. When the state police attempted to raid some of the best-known casinos along Central Avenue they had difficulty locating Circuit Court Judge Plummer Dobbs, as required, to get a search warrant. When they eventually found him at the Hot Springs Country Club, he peppered them with questions until he found a way to avoid issuing the warrant because of an incorrectly prepared affidavit. Dobbs would later say that some of the state policemen seeking the warrant were known to be willing patrons of the very clubs they came to raid.

Dobbs continued to use technical excuses to delay matters another week before he issued a search warrant. By then the gaming tables and equipment had all been removed from the offending nightclubs. Faubus's state police would continue similar raids, with similar results, over the next two years until 1966 when a new governor would be elected.

The defeat of the gambling amendment in the 1964 general election compelled Faubus to articulate a public rationalization for his hands-off policy. Accordingly, he claimed to be worried that the state police could be hit with civil suits for false arrest if the raids proved to be unjustified. He reasoned, therefore, that anyone with complaints against an alleged casino should first notify local authorities that could then invite the state police to become involved if they felt that it was advisable. While arguing his preference for reserving the participation of state lawmen as an option for local authorities to decide, he explained, "If, for example, Winthrop Rockefeller became governor I don't want him to send state police to [my hometown of] Huntsville to take over the elections."

In reality, Garland County's anti-gambling local enforcement was a sham. After a four-month investigation, a Hot Springs grand jury declared in September 1965 that there was no basis for action against the private clubs. The jury even strayed so far from reality as to commend the local police for their vigilant efforts.[139]

Meanwhile illegal gambling was taking root in Pulaski County around Little Rock and its suburbs. Since the capital city's metropolitan area was seven times larger than nearby Hot Springs it had long accounted for a significant share of the smaller town's gaming patrons. Pulaski County entrepreneurs with a sense of adventure, and a talent for influencing local law enforcement officials, started building gaming facilities in the Little Rock area. Most notable among them was the Club Westwood, which was constructed in the mid-1950's about five miles beyond the city limits on the road to Hot Springs.

The club's brightly lighted entrance resembled the Las Vegas style complete with a lush red carpet where doormen greeted elegantly dressed guests. Like The Vapors it had a first class dining room with starched white linen tablecloths. A polished maple dance floor and bandstand for live musicians filled out the dining area. But the main attraction was the salon beyond a distinctive orange door toward the back of the dining room. It contained a small casino like the one at The Vapors. Guests who could thrill at their winnings, or lament their losses, might see each other sitting in the pews at church or temple the next day. Also like The Vapors, the Westwood had its own chips and dice. Owner Barney Levine promotionally imprinted the chips and dice with both the club name and his given name in distinctive gold script.

Presumably Levine had arranged an agreement with Pulaski County authorities that resembled the one in Hot Springs. Although fined many times he never spent a night in jail and his customers were invariably untouched by the police. Levine may have also been a horse bookmaker as well. A U.S. Senate committee investigating bookie wire services called him to testify in 1962. He revealed nothing by taking the Fifth Amendment. Like Madden in Hot Springs, Levine gave generously to Little Rock area charities.[140]

Early in 1966 Governor Faubus announced he would not seek a seventh term. His polling showed that voters felt he had been in power too long. Moreover, if he did choose to run he assumed that Rockefeller would again be his opponent in 1966. Given Rockefeller's wealth, respectable showing in 1964 and the polling results noted above, Faubus did not think he could beat Rockefeller in a rematch.[141]

---

128 Sidney McMath, *Promises Kept*, 286, 289-90; James Pierce, "From McMath to Rockefeller: Arkansas Governors and Illegal Gambling in Postwar Hot Springs, 1945-1970," 18, 26

129 Bernard Land and Myrick Land, *A Short History of Las Vegas* (Reno: University of Nevada Press, 1999), 97-99; Richard Sasuly, Bookies and Bettors, 234-36

130 T. J. English, *Havana Nocturne*, 86, 91, 94-96, , 109, 269; Carl Sifakis, *The Mafia Encyclopedia*, 35, 214

131 Roy Reed, *Orval Faubus: The Life and Times of an American Prodigal*, 318; James Pierce, "From McMath to Rockefeller: Arkansas Governors and Illegal Gambling in Postwar Hot Springs, 1945-1970," 32, 35; Wallace Turner, "Hot Springs: Gamblers' Haven," *New York Times*, March 8, 1964, available https://goo.gl/dcrZzh [Accessed July 7, 2017]

132 Orval Allbritton, *Lawman: The Story of Clay White* (Hot Springs, Ark.: Garland Country Historical Society, 2014), 120, 162; Robert Boyle, "The Hottest Spring in Hot Springs," *Sports Illustrated*, March 19, 1962, available http://on.si.com/2tzoHI8 [Accessed July 12, 2017]; James Pierce, "From McMath to Rockefeller: Arkansas Governors and Illegal Gambling in Postwar Hot Springs, 1945-1970," 38; Orval Allbritton, *Leo and Verne*, 588-89; Michael Hodge, "Vapors," *Encyclopedia of Arkansas History and Culture*, February 24, 2014, available http://bit.ly/2t4eOF4 [Accessed July 12, 2017]; Roy Reed, *Orval Faubus: The Life and Times of an American Prodigal*, 215, 318; Central Distributors ,"About Us," available http://bit.ly/2tf2oFO [Accessed July 12, 2107]

133 Graham Nown, *Arkansas Godfather*, 341

134 Selwyn Rabb, *Five Families: The Rise, Decline and Resurgence of America's Most Powerful Mafia Empires*, 122-23, 127-28, 136-37; James Pierce, "From McMath to Rockefeller: Arkansas Governors and Illegal Gambling in Postwar Hot Springs, 1945-1970," 42; Colonel Lynn Davis, *They Said it Couldn't be Done* (Little Rock, Ark.: Davis Creek Press, 2009), 170, 172

135 Wallace Turner, "Hot Springs: Gamblers' Haven," *New York Times*, March 8, 1964

136 Ray Hanley, *A Place Apart: A Pictorial History of Hot Springs*, Arkansas, 137

137 *Ibid.*, 135; James Pierce, "From McMath to Rockefeller," 46; Orval Allbritton, *Lawman: The Story of Clay White*, 118-19; John Ward, *The Arkansas Rockefeller* (Baton Rouge: Louisiana State University Press, 1978), 35

138 John Ward, *The Arkansas Rockefeller*, 39-41, 48, 50; James Pierce, "From McMath to Rockefeller," 51

139 James Pierce, "From McMath to Rockefeller," 52-54, 63-66, 70;

140 Jim Pfeifer, "You Bet", *Facebook: History of the Heights*, available http://bit.ly/2sQJSUU [Accessed July 12, 2017]

141 James Pierce, "From McMath to Rockefeller," 68

Chapter Ten
GAME OVER

DESPITE LOSING THE 1964 gubernatorial election to Orval Faubus, Winthrop Rockefeller was sufficiently pleased with his 44% share of the vote to announce immediately thereafter that he would run again in 1966. Both men realized that the growing number of voters who wanted to give up the futile fight for racial segregation would increasingly be drawn to Rockefeller during a rematch.

Partly to win incremental support from voters concerned with another issue, therefore, Rockefeller repeatedly assailed the governor for his failure to end illegal gambling. After Faubus announced that he would not run for a seventh term, the state's Democratic Party nominated a strong segregationist, thereby enabling Rockefeller to win the 1966 general election with a combination of moderate white voters and about 95% of the black vote. Although ending the segregation fight was the chief campaign issue, Rockefeller's repetitious pledges since the end of the 1964 to shut down illegal gambling if elected in 1966 was at least a high profile secondary one.

The day after his January 10, 1967, inauguration, however, Rockefeller curiously said that he expected local authorities to take care of the gambling problem. That led reporters to question him the next day at a news conference when he clarified, "If gambling again becomes flagrant ... I will move of my own initiative." Early in February he sent the state police on hunting expeditions to discover if illegal gambling in Garland and Pulaski counties was as flagrant as recent press reports had suggested. During one weekend the troopers visited a variety of establishments where they found nearly forty blackjack tables, a dozen crap tables, two roulette wheels and hundreds of slot machines.

As a result, the governor sent letters to law enforcement organizations in the two counties, as well as the mayors of Hot Springs and North Little Rock, giving them until 27 February to close down any gambling operations in their jurisdictions. The letter concluded by warning that any such business remaining open after the deadline was subject to state police raids. Thus, on 28 February Rockefeller told state police director, Colonel Herman Lindsey, to take whatever action was necessary to eliminate illegal gambling throughout the state. Since the governor realized that Lindsey might have been a source of the habitual advance raid warnings that casinos received during the Faubus era, Rockefeller announced that Lindsey was on probation until the end of April.

Meanwhile four state senators introduced a bill to permit state supervised gambling on a local option basis. The resulting bill proposed to create a state crime commission to police and license gaming clubs. There were to be five commissioners appointed by the governor with the consent of the senate. In order to enforce the applicable laws, the commission would be empowered to carry out investigations and subpoena witnesses. The bill would authorize no more than one casino per 15,000 residents in the affected counties. It also stipulated that the state would collect an annual $10,000 license fee from each business as well as a tax of 8% of its gross revenues.

In early March, the bill passed both chambers of the Arkansas legislature by the narrowest of margins. For several days its sponsors expected that Rockefeller would either sign it, or let it become law without his signature. On 8 March, however, he vetoed the bill. The sponsors immediately charged that Rockefeller had broken his word to them. All four claimed that they would never have introduced the bill if the governor had not privately indicated weeks earlier that he would let the bill become law should it get through the legislature. Other legislators who voted for the bill also claimed that they would not have done so except for rumors of the governor's acquiescence, if not direct support. After the veto, a number of legislators that voted "Yea" renounced their votes in order to remain on the popular side of statewide public sentiment.

Governor Winthrop Rockefeller | Arkansas Governors: Official Portrait

In response to accusations that Rockefeller broke his word, the governor denied that he ever promised to support the bill. He even claimed that he was unaware of it until it was formally introduced. He speculated that the misunderstanding might have resulted from an earlier meeting with selected legislators and others in which methods of revitalizing the Hot Springs economy were discussed. Although the meeting included conversations about the possibility of legalizing gambling, it also contained discussion about changing the laws governing mixed alcoholic drinks, which were also generally prohibited in Arkansas. Rockefeller replied to a proposal on the latter topic by saying that he would send it to an aide for further study. He did not, he avowed, make any definite statement about his stance on legitimatizing gambling.[142]

The first sign of defiance against Rockefeller's enforcement materialized with Hot Springs Municipal Judge Earl Mazander shortly after the state police raids started. Specifically, he ordered that all gambling equipment seized and taken to Little Rock during an 11 March raid be turned over to the Hot Springs police chief. Although the state police partly complied by sending some of the items intended for use as evidence to Hot Springs, Mazander issued an arrest warrant for the state trooper that led the raid. While the judge was eventually persuaded to dismiss the case, he ordered that no evidence captured on future raids could be removed from Garland County without the consent of local authorities.

Next, Q. Byrum Hurst, who had become a state senator, introduced a bill to abolish the Criminal Investigative Division (CID) of the state police, which was the enforcement arm Rockefeller was using to raid the illegal businesses. Hurst dubiously suggested that the state's highways were becoming unsafe because too many troopers were involved in anti-gambling activities. Traffic fatality statistics later discredited Hurst's allegation when they revealed that Arkansas might have been the only state in the country to report a decline in traffic deaths in 1967. After Hurst's bill was voted down he tried to tack it onto the state police appropriations bill, but the legislature also rejected that tactic.

During April, Garland County authorities decided it was better to pretend to be cooperating with the governor rather than resisting. Thus, Sheriff Bud Canada assisted state troopers on a number of raids. In May he told reporters that he would "use the full facilities of [his] office to carry out this [enforcement] policy," concluding insincerely, "as I have in the past." He did not clarify that some of the seized gaming equipment supposedly stored in his office was trickling back into circulation instead of being destroyed as intended.

In June Governor Rockefeller conceded that illegal gambling was mysteriously returning to Hot Springs even after the raids. After futilely asking that local authorities increase their vigilance, he reasoned that the state police would need to become even more involved. Equally important, he concluded that the state organization needed a new commander.

Lindsey had basically failed his probation. For the preceding twenty years the colonel had become habituated to erratic anti-gaming law enforcement, which fluctuated from governor to governor and year to year. Given such a pattern, casino owners too readily presumed that Lindsey's enforcement under Rockefeller would also prove to be only temporary. Therefore, Rockefeller announced before the end of June that an outsider would replace Lindsey, who decided to retire.[143]

Early in 1967 Arkansas native and thirty-three-year-old FBI agent Lynn Davis requested a transfer from Los Angeles to Little Rock in order to be closer to his ailing mother. Before the Bureau acted on the request a previous college classmate, who worked for Rockefeller and was aware that the governor was looking for a newcomer to lead the state police, contacted Davis. About two weeks later Davis met with Rockefeller in Little Rock. The day after Davis returned to Los Angeles the governor phoned him to offer him the top slot at the Arkansas State Police. Davis eagerly accepted.

Although Davis would take decisive action against the gambling businesses, he would also face entrenched resistance and unexpected obstacles. Even before he arrived his appointment provoked resentments among some incumbent state police employees and politicos who benefitted from the habitual corrupt methods of enforcing anti-gaming laws. Since nothing in his seven years at the FBI suggested that he was unqualified to accept Rockefeller's offer, gambling interests looked for other ways block Davis. The first one took the form of a technical objection raised by Democratic Attorney General Joe Purcell.

Colonel Lynn Davis – 1967 | Arkansas State Police

Specifically, Arkansas law required that anyone appointed as director of the state police had to have been a state resident for the preceding ten years. The requirement was adopted shortly after World War II in order to protect Colonel Lindsey who might otherwise have been displaced by a returning war veteran since former soldiers were popularly respected among the public, as the GI Revolt in Hot Springs would demonstrate.

Rockefeller responded to Purcell by noting that Davis had always remained an Arkansan at heart and was therefore eligible. Surprisingly, an initial court ruling upheld the governor's liberal interpretation. But Purcell promptly appealed the case, which would eventually land at the state Supreme Court. Nonetheless, Davis took his oath of office on 1 August and stated that he would not accept a salary while his qualifications were under appeal. He added, however, that he would not let doubts about his eligibility inhibit his plans to act.

Since Davis could not know how long the appeal might take, he quickly moved against the gamblers. His first objective was to destroy gambling equipment instead of arresting casino owners or customers. Gaming could not continue if the equipment was demolished, whereas the prosecution of alleged violators was subject to delays and uncertainties through a historically corrupted legal process. Once the gaming equipment was destroyed, any attempts to replace it from sources outside the state would likely trigger violations of interstate commerce laws, thereby authorizing additional enforcement by federal marshals and FBI agents.

His first raid took place in Hot Springs less than three weeks after taking office and was executed without notifying local authorities. After plainclothes officers observed gambling at four casinos, Colonel Davis placed men at parade rest in front of the building entrances to prevent any equipment from being removed. Next he surprised the local prosecuting attorney at one-thirty in the morning with a request for the search and seizure warrants required to raid the businesses. As a result, gaming equipment was confiscated at each location.

Unfortunately, the troopers were not permitted to destroy the captured gear because the warrants only authorized search and seizure. Consequently, the colonel turned the equipment over to Hot Springs officials who were expected to destroy it. In later raids Davis would be angered to learn that at least some of the relinquished gear had been recycled to other casinos instead of destroyed.

Unsurprisingly, Sheriff Canada was incensed that Davis did not seek local cooperation during the August raid. But despite the sheriff's complaint Davis remained firmly resolved to exclude Canada's men in future raids as well. In a 2008 interview near the end of his life, Davis indicated that he did not know anyone in a position of authority in Garland County at the time who was trustworthy.

Davis's raiders returned to Hot Springs in October and confiscated $250,000 worth of slot machines. They also located secret casino equipment repair shops where they found one hundred functioning machines and parts enough to build an additional two hundred and fifty. A rental truck full of slots was also captured. When the machines in the truck were destroyed Davis discovered from some of the serial numbers that almost twenty of the slots had been seized in earlier raids but never demolished as intended.

Angered by the discovery that gaming equipment was being redeployed instead of demolished, Davis decided to openly pinpoint the responsible Garland County enforcement officials.

Colonel Lynn Davis With Slot Machines | Arkansas State Police

During an October address to a Little Rock civic group he accused the Hot Springs police chief and his assistant of helping the casinos. Moreover, he warned that if a Garland County grand jury would not indict the two men, he would take matters into his own hands. The speech triggered the Hot Springs Civil Service Commission to urge an investigation. Since Judge Mazander was presiding, he predictably concluded that Davis's accusations were based on rumors instead of facts.

Nonetheless, Davis's well-publicized raids and his rising public profile seemed to be promoting a new resolve in favor of enforcement throughout many of the state's localities. For example, local authorities confiscated about twenty slots long known to be operating at clubs on North College Avenue in Fayetteville where the University of Arkansas is located.

Before long both Davis and Rockefeller received death threats. In early December the police chief of San Angelo, Texas, notified Arkansas authorities that a prisoner claimed to know of a plot to assassinate Rockefeller. At least one newspaper reported that the prisoner told a Texas official that Hot Springs gamblers intended to kill Rockefeller by sabotaging one of his jet planes. Upon investigation Lynn Davis dismissed the San Angelo threat as mere jailhouse talk. Nonetheless, he indirectly messaged the Hot Springs underworld that there would be revenge if any attempts were made on his life, or the governor's. He even hinted that Rockefeller had already contracted for vigilante justice in case of such an eventuality. Lest there be any doubt about the vengeance, Lynn hinted that the vigilante justice might be performed through contracts with underworld figures instead of the state police.[144]

Although the colonel downplayed the Texas rumor, Davis recalled years later that the governor did, in fact, once come close to losing his life in an airplane accident. It happened on a flight to Memphis with his staff. As the plane approached the airport Rockefeller's Falcon Jet pilot was unable to lower the landing gear. The jet burned low on fuel as the crew tried repeatedly, but unsuccessfully, to lower the wheels. Without them, the pilot would need to try a belly landing, which could easily end with fiery deaths for everyone on board.

Eventually, someone suggested that the crew phone the manufacturer for recommendations while the plane circled to exhaust its fuel. Sure enough, Falcon personnel said that the crew could lower the gear with a manual crank after removing a metal plate on the floor to get at the mechanism. Although ripping up the carpet gave them access to the floorboard, they had no screwdriver to remove the metal plate. Fortunately, a dime proved to be a satisfactory substitute and the landing gear was cranked down manually after the floorboard was removed.[145]

Perhaps because he sensed that his residency status appeal would be decided against him, Davis continued to move quickly and relentlessly to stamp out illegal gambling before he might be told to vacate his office. It was too much to expect that the politicos who secretly benefitted from the status quo for so long would watch silently while their ox was gored. The inevitable front-page confrontation unexpectedly occurred in Little Rock instead of Hot Springs.

Partly to placate resentment in Garland Country, undercover troopers soon raided eleven clubs in Pulaski County, which encompasses Little Rock and suburbs such as North Little Rock. At Barney Levine's Club Westwood, for example, the raiders discovered 30,000 pairs of dice. In a suburb near that club they found a semitrailer full of gambling equipment that was supposed to have been confiscated by Hot Springs police.

Over the years prior to Davis's Pulaski County raid the eleven Little Rock area bookies had been charged a total of 118 times with gambling related felonies but the charges were generally reduced to misdemeanors and sometimes dropped altogether. As a result, over ninety percent of the time the ensuing fines were only fifty dollars. Since the habitual pattern strongly implied a corrupt legal apparatus, Davis told a group of Little Rock business leaders during a speech, "[I]t is time we insisted again that law enforcement officers, prosecuting attorneys, judges, and juries do their duty."

His complaint annoyed prosecuting attorney Jim Adkisson who was assigned to the grand jury investigating the eleven bookies. As a result, Adkisson told Davis to disclose the name of the informant who had told the colonel about the Pulaski County gambling locations. On 5 December he called Davis before the grand jury where the colonel was repeatedly asked to reveal the name, but he repetitively declined. After several iterations, the jury foreman turned to Adkisson and said, "If he will not tell us the name...let's take him before the judge. The judge will make him tell."

Addressing Davis, Adkisson said, "Colonel, I am just going to have to take you before the judge to order you to tell us your informant."

Davis replied, "Surely you have enough [evidence] to make a good case...without knowing the name of the informant."

Adkisson did not reply but merely took Davis into the courtroom where Circuit Court Judge William Kirby addressed the colonel, "The prosecutor tells me you will not give him the name of your informant." Davis confirmed the validity of the statement but again said he would not provide the name. Kirby then made a technical error by failing to ask Davis to give the name to him (the judge) as opposed to Adkission, and held Davis in contempt of court for declining to tell Adkisson. Kirby told the bailiff to put Davis in a prison cell until he was ready to divulge the name to the prosecutor.

Public reaction soon demonstrated that Adkisson and Kirby had overplayed their hand. The Associated Press later listed the colonel's incarceration as the top news story out of Arkansas that year, ranking it even higher than Rockefeller's election as the state's first Republican governor in a hundred years. *The New York Times* interviewed Davis over a prison pay phone. The chairman of a chiefs-of-police lobbying organization in Washington, D. C., wrote a letter supporting Davis. Governor Rockefeller asked the Arkansas State Supreme Court for an emergency ruling the next morning.

The Supreme Court overruled Judge Kirby on the technicality that he failed to ask Davis to reveal the name to him and had instead instructed Davis to disclose it to the prosecutor. The essentially comical distinction was good enough to get Davis released without bail after only a single night in jail. Rockefeller staged a press conference at the jailhouse upon Davis's release, pledging his full support for the director. He labeled Kirby's action as political harassment that nobody but gamblers and criminals could celebrate.

But less than three weeks later the state Supreme Court ruled against Davis on the residency matter. Since the decision basically rendered Davis ineligible to be state police director, he was forced to vacate his office on December 23, 1967.

Despite the ruling, the publicity from Davis's brief imprisonment and the corruption implied by it proved to be a turning point in the battle against illegal gambling in Arkansas. Rockefeller replaced Davis with an assistant director who proved to be a caretaker for a year before retiring. Next the governor selected another outsider. This one had twenty-eight years of FBI experience and renewed Davis's aggressive enforcement. A final indication that sentiment had turned decisively against illegal gambling came in 1969 when a Hot Springs grand jury indicted twenty-five residents for gaming violations.[146]

Although Lynn Davis was director of the Arkansas state police for less than five months he effectively ended illegal gambling in the state. He could not have done it without Rockefeller's commitment, which partly reflected the governor's financial independence. There was not enough money in the state to turn his head.[147]

Lynn Davis Jailed | Courtesy of Ray Hanley

Soon after Davis was forced out of office, Rockefeller hired him privately to help conduct an investigation into alleged abuse of prisoners at the state's prison farms. Although circumstances were bad enough, they were not as awful as depicted in the Hollywood movie, *Brubaker*, which was inspired by exaggerated narratives of the authentic situation. The true problems resulted from parsimonious efforts to minimize the cost of operating prisons by permitting trusties to function as prison guard assistants. When the trusty system was abolished many trusties tried to escape. They feared for their lives because the ordinary prisoners hated them.

Following the prison investigation Davis became director of the governor's crime commission. He advised Rockefeller on reorganizing the National Guard, the Alcohol Beverage Control Board and other agencies. Before Rockefeller left office in January 1971 the governor persuaded President Richard Nixon to appoint Davis as the U. S. Marshal for eastern Arkansas where he remained five years. Davis earned a law degree while in the marshal service and thereafter became a practicing attorney for about thirty years.[148]

---

[142] James Pierce, "From McMath to Rockefeller: Arkansas Governors and Illegal Gambling in Postwar Hot Springs, 1945-1970," 69-73; Cathy Urwin, *Agenda For Reform: Winthrop Rockefeller as Governor of Arkansas, 1967-71* (Fayetteville: University of Arkansas Press, 1991), 56, 107-8

[143] James Pierce, "From McMath to Rockefeller," 74-77; Lynn Davis, "Arkansas State Police Project." Interviewed by Michael Lindsey. *Pryor Center for Arkansas Oral and Visual History: University of Arkansas Libraries*, August 18, 2003, PDF Download available http://bit.ly/2ukjh75 [Accessed July 12, 2017], 23

[144] James Pierce, "From McMath to Rockefeller," 77-85; Lynn Davis, "Arkansas State Police Project." Interviewed by Michael Lindsey, 4, 8, 19

[145] Colonel Lynn Davis, *They Said it Couldn't be Done*, 188-89

[146] James Pierce, "From McMath to Rockefeller," 86-87, 90; Colonel Lynn Davis, *They Said it Couldn't be Done*, 191; Lynn Davis, "Arkansas State Police Project." Interviewed by Michael Lindsey, 5, 13-15

[147] Lynn Davis, "Arkansas State Police Project.," Interviewed by Michael Lindsey. 5

[148] *Ibid.*, 19, 21

Chapter Eleven
Memoir

I BECAME A TEENAGER in Little Rock two months before John F. Kennedy was elected president in 1960. Together with my three siblings we had lived in the town all our lives and resided with mom who divorced dad five years earlier when she was thirty-seven years old. She remained a divorcee and dated a number of men before wedding her second husband in 1971. During Kennedy's presidency I learned that some of her dates took her to Hot Springs, mostly during Oaklawn Park's horse racing season when Arkansas was in the process of shaking off winter.

Like many others in Little Rock, we warmed our house on the remaining cold days of the season with natural gas heaters. Since the one in my bedroom did not have a pilot light, I had to light it with a match each time I used it. On one such occasion I recall first noticing matches mom gave me were enclosed in a distinctive yellow and orange cardboard matchbook overprinted with the image of a pair of thespian masks and inscribed with "The Vapors" in script.

When curiosity led me to ask her about the matchbook, mom answered, "The Vapors is a nightclub in Hot Springs. Mr. Portland and I went there for dinner after a day at the races."

"A nightclub?" I asked. "I thought those were only in big cities like New York and Chicago ... You know, like in the movies."

"Well, that's mostly true, but Hot Springs is an exception."

"Why?"

"Oh, the ones in Hot Springs have gambling."

"You like to gamble?"

"No. No, not really. It's mostly for the men. I just like the dinners and the shows."

"What shows?"

"Floor shows. You know, singers like Frank Sinatra."

"You mean Frank Sinatra visits Hot Springs?"

"No; less famous singers. People you wouldn't know at your age."

The explanation must have satisfied me because I don't remember learning anything more about Hot Springs gambling from mom.

Over the next four years, however, I realized that some of my public school classmates had gradually become familiar with gambling. By the eleventh or twelfth grade I'd hear discussions in the school hallways and lunchroom by boys boasting half furtively about their underage visits to Oaklawn Park.

An exclusive sect even talked expertly about neighborhood poker games where Dave Brubeck jazz selections such as *Take Five* played in the background and cigarette smoke rose from most of the seats around the poker table to gradually transform the room into one resembling the scene in *The Hustler* when George C. Scott's character first appears on screen. My classmates normally played seven-card stud, which was popular long before Texas Hold'em became the rage. Within a few years *The Cincinnati Kid* became the signature poker movie of the era. The highest compliment a student player could earn when I later got to college was to be called "The Man." It was the nickname for the venerable Edward G. Robinson character who beat Steve McQueen's youthful character in a stud game showdown to end the movie.

During my senior high school year I tagged along to Oaklawn with a couple of experienced classmates on a few occasions. I normally couldn't afford any bets larger than two-dollar "show" tickets and rarely bought a "win" ticket because of the higher loss probability. Although I typically lost the full amount of my budget by the end of the day, the thrill I felt at the end of the few races when I had a winning ticket led me to appreciate how track regulars might become gambling addicts. I never tried to enter one of the casinos, partly because I was underage, but mostly because I didn't have enough money. Like Meyer Lansky, I realized that gambling wasn't for me. Ironically, however, about a dozen years later I landed on Wall Street, the biggest and most addictive casino of all.

Thus, in my early teens I learned that Arkansas politicians winked at illegal gaming. Since it seemed irrelevant to my life, I gave it little thought. I may have even assumed that the practice was common all across the country. I don't recall neighborhood adults, or their children who were my peers, ever explicitly discussing the likely corrupting influence on government. At most, I overheard only vague hints beyond which the speaker would elaborate no further. Finally, I was completely unaware for decades thereafter of the gaming clubs around Little Rock. Nonetheless, the sinister side of the status quo became obvious when I was sixteen and the bomb exploded at The Vapors. It was front-page news all across the state.

The underworld attack on The Vapors was about ten months before the November 1963 Kennedy Assassination that left Americans emotionally stunned. But a week after the president's funeral his young widow provided a morally uplifting metaphor that would transform the 1960s.

During a *Life Magazine* interview she revealed that Jack's favorite Broadway show had been *Camelot*. She told the interviewer that her husband particularly liked the couplet, "Don't ever let it be forgot, that once there was a spot, for one brief shining moment, that was Camelot." As an idealist, she added, President Kennedy particularly liked the Camelot legend because he interpreted history as something that could be shaped by heroes like King Arthur. "There will be great presidents again," she said, "but there will never be another Camelot."[149]

Suddenly many Americans imagined the Kennedy era to be exactly as she described it. Hence, they hungered to recapture it by reshaping the entire country into the idealistic mold implied by the metaphor. As a result, Kennedy brothers Robert and Ted were presidential contenders for years thereafter, chiefly because of their family connection. President Lyndon Johnson considered it a duty to act as Kennedy's political executor, which partly explains the 1964 Civil Rights Act and the Great Society initiative.

The nation's impressionable youth were among the most impacted by the Camelot spirit. Future President Bill Clinton was among them. After a brief flirtation with Barry Goldwater's right-wing politics, Hillary Rodham (Clinton) also migrated swiftly to the left. One of my high school friends who sold newspaper subscriptions the summer after Kennedy's death told me that almost every black family home he entered had a portrait of John Kennedy displayed prominently on a wall or table.

Winthrop Rockefeller's election as governor in 1966 demonstrated that a surprising number of Arkansans were similarly impacted. First, and foremost, it indicated that the state had turned away from Jim Crow, as would Georgia four years later when Jimmy Carter was elected governor of that most influential of all deep-south states. Second, partly because the spirit of Camelot suggested that it was time to elect a governor who could not be corrupted, Arkansans chose one whose personal wealth made him invulnerable to bribery.

Many years later novelist Stephen Hunter sparked my interest to learn the truth about the Hot Springs legend. Since reading his novel, *Hot Springs,* seventeen years ago, I've been curious to learn how much of his story was true. Merely by growing up in Little Rock when I did, I knew much of it was hyperbolic fiction, which he forthrightly confessed in the book's acknowledgements.

Presumably Hunter appreciates Hollywood director John Ford's story-telling dictum: "When given a choice between the truth and the legend, print the legend." I've long been a fan of Hunter's Bob Lee Swagger and Earl Swagger stories, partially because he is one of the few popular authors to portray fictional Arkansans as something more than hayseeds. His prime character in a string of plot-connected novels, Bob Lee Swagger, is modeled after Carlos Hathcock who was America's top sniper during the Vietnam War.[150]

Like World War II hero Audie Murphy, as a boy Hathcock helped feed his family by shooting small game. While Murphy came of age on an east Texas farm, the youthful Hathcock lived on the outskirts of Little Rock, which was the state's largest city. But the west end of the town is on high ground cut with numerous ravines that were heavily wooded when Hathcock and I were boys. I recall, albeit rarely, seeing other boys shoot squirrels and similar game along some of the creeks.

Hunter's Bob Lee Swagger novels accurately portray the mannerisms of the best among Vietnam veterans who grew up as poor whites in the South and were teenagers when Elvis Presley transformed popular music. *Hot Springs* is Stephen Hunter's story about Bob Lee's fictional dad when the father joined McMath's GI Revolt in order to reform the local government so that critics might never again disparage the place as "The Devil's Town."

The End

---

[149] James Pierson, "How Jackie Kennedy Invented the Camelot Legend After JFK's Death," *Daily Beast*, November 12, 2013, available http://thebea.st/2sZkMDa [July 14, 2017]

[150] Sean O'Connor, "John Ford (1894-1973)," *100 People Who Changed 20th Century America*, ed. Mary Cross (Santa Barbara, Cal.: ABC-CLIO, 2013), 146

BIBLIOGRAPHIC ESSAY

RESEARCH FOR *THE DEVIL'S TOWN* required sources for each of three components needed to tell the story of the gangster era. First were matters specific to Hot Springs. Examples include the town's political, law enforcement, criminal and illegal-gaming operations. Second were the factors that weaved the town's libertine history into the concurrent national experience. Third were those that described the fluctuating relationships between the political and enforcement authorities of the state of Arkansas to those local to Hot Springs.

Some sources overlapped, but many fell into only one of the three categories. In a sector awash with unreliable and sensationalized accounts, Selwyn Raab's *Five Families,* Thomas Reppetto's *American Mafia,* Bryan Burrough's *Public Enemies* and Graham Nown's *Arkansas Godfather* proved to be generally dependable sources for understanding how seemingly isolated Hot Springs incidents fit into the larger setting of the American Mafia.

Orval Allbritton's *Leo and Verne* is an example of a source that touched multiple categories. Although it provides a wealth of facts and anecdotes specific to Hot Springs during the twenty-year McLaughlin rule from 1927 to 1947, it also documents the variable relationships between the Machine and the six governors of the era. Biographies of governors McMath, Faubus, and Rockefeller by Jim Lester, Roy Reed and John Ward, respectively, illuminate how the growing encroachment of state authority ultimately ended illegal gambling. Predictably, Lester's McMath biography is a useful source about the Veterans Revolt.

Chapter-by-chapter summaries are detailed below.

The introductory chapter draws upon Wallace Turner's "Hot Springs: Gambler's Haven" in the March 8, 1964, *New York Times* and Robert Boyle's "The Hottest Spring in Hot Springs" from the March 19, 1962, *Sports Illustrated* to paint a picture of the town's gambling ambiance shortly before it was eclipsed by Las Vegas. Dee Brown's *The American Spa: Hot Springs Arkansas* (Little Rock, Ark.: Rose Publishing, 1962) and Francis Scully's *Hot Springs Arkansas and Hot Springs National Park* (Little Rock, Ark.: Pioneer Press, 1962) provide background on the town as a center for hydrotherapy and gambling as well as its status as a safe haven for criminals. Two good sources for the situational background on the American Mafia were Selwyn Raab's *Five Families: The Rise, Decline and Resurgence of America's Most Powerful Mafia Empires* (New York: St. Martin's Press, 2006) and Thomas Reppetto's *American Mafia: A History of its Rise and Power* (New York: Henry Holt & Company, 2004).

Gangster Owney Madden's assimilation into the community following his move to Hot Springs from New York in 1935 is described in the second chapter. It draws upon Graham Nown's *Arkansas Godfather* (Little Rock, Ark.: Butler Center Books, 2011) and Orval Albritton's *Leo and Verne* (Hot Springs, Ark.: Garland County Historical Society, 2003) to describe the local political and illegal-gaming structure when Madden arrived.

The Last Testament of Lucky Luciano (New York: Random House, 1981) by Martin Gosch and Richard Hammer summarizes the capture and extradition of Mob kingpin Charles "Lucky" Luciano narrated in chapter three. Other sources include the books by Raab, Nown, Albritton, and Reppetto, noted above.

Chapter four integrates the stories of such superficially disconnected events as the 1933 Kansas City Massacre, the kidnappings of the Hamm and Schmidt brewery heirs that same year, and FBI Director J. Edgar Hoover's 1936 contrived capture of the only Public Enemy Number One ever taken alive by revealing their connections to Hot Springs. A unified narrative was derived from sources such as William Helmer's and Rick Mattix's *Public Enemies: America's Criminal Past 1919-1940* (New York: Checkmark Books, 1998), Peter Burrough's *Public Enemies* (New York: Penguin Group, 2004), Robert Underhill's *Criminals and Folk Heroes* (New York: Algora Publishing, 2015), and Don Whitehead's *The FBI Story* (New York: Random House, 1956).

Chapter five's analysis of how Leo McLaughlin and Verne Ledgerwood came into power in Hot Springs after 1927 is derived from Allbritton's *Leo and Verne* and Walter Davenport's "Sin Takes a Hot Bath" from *Colliers Weekly* magazine in the issue of August 8, 1931.

The description of life under the McLaughlin Machine in chapter six relies upon *Leo and Verne* and Graham Nown's *Arkansas Godfather* as well as William J. Clinton's *My Life* (New York: Random House, 2004), T. J. Weeks' *Havana Nocturne* (New York: William Morrow, 2007) and Shirley Abbott's *The Bookmaker's Daughter: A Memory Unbound* (Fayetteville: University of Arkansas Press, 2006).

The irony that a major illegal gambling center emerged on the buckle of the Bible Belt is investigated in chapter seven. Among the sources for analyzing the region's contrasting economic and religious characteristics where the Assemblies of God Church was organized in 1914 are Ray Hanley's *A Place Apart* (Fayetteville: University of Arkansas Press, 2011) and Edith Blumhofer's *The Assemblies of God: A Popular History* (Springfield, Mo.: Radiant Books, 1985) as well as economic statistics from the Federal Reserve Bank of St. Louis.

The Veterans Revolt that resulted in the overthrow of McLaughlin's Machine in 1947 and described in chapter eight relies upon Patsy Ramsey's "A Place at the Table: Hot Springs and the GI Revolt," (*Arkansas Historical Quarterly*, V. 59, N. 4, Winter 2000), to document how fraudulent poll tax receipts had been used to sustain the political Machine and how the slate of GI candidates exposed poll tax fraud in order to win the 1946 elections. Biographies on Sid McMath such as his *Promises Kept* (Fayetteville: University of Arkansas Press, 2003) autobiography and Jim Lester's *A Man For Arkansas* (Little Rock, Ar.: Rose Publishing, 1976), contributed to the GI Revolt narrative. Also helpful was a 2008 Master's Thesis by University of Arkansas student Jim Pierce titled, "From McMath to Rockefeller: Arkansas Governors and Illegal Gambling in Postwar Hot Springs 1945-1970."

Chapter nine analyzes the economic aftermath of the gambling hiatus that followed the GI Revolt noted above. Shirley Abbott's *Bookmaker's Daughter* documents the challenging adjustment required of a typical family that had relied upon illegal gaming to provide a living during the McLaughlin era. The increasing gambling-center competition to Hot Springs from Las Vegas and Havana is put into context by Bernard and Myrick Land's *A Short History of Las Vegas* (Reno: University of Nevada Press, 1999), Richard Sasuly's *Bookies and Bettors* (New York: Holt, Reinhart, and Winston, 1982), and T. J. Weeks' *Havana Nocturne* noted above. Valuable information regarding the relationships between Hot Springs and governors Faubus and Rockefeller is found in Roy Reed's *Faubus: The Life and Times of an American Prodigal* (Fayetteville, Ark.: University of Arkansas Press, 1997) and John Ward's *The Arkansas Rockefeller* (Baton Rouge: Louisiana State University Press, 1978).

The end of Arkansas's illegal gaming in 1967 is narrated in chapter ten. Among the best sources were Jim Pierce's "From McMath to Rockefeller: Arkansas Governors and Illegal Gambling in Postwar Hot Springs, 1945-1970" and Colonel Lynn Davis, *They Said it Couldn't be Done* (Little Rock, Ark.: Davis Creek Press, 2009). Other works cited were Cathy Urwin's *Agenda For Reform: Winthrop Rockefeller as Governor of Arkansas* (Fayetteville: University of Arkansas Press, 1991) and an interview of Lynn Davis by Michael Lindsey of the *Arkansas State Police Project* on August 18, 2003.

The preceding chapter-by-chapter summary only highlights some the more prominent sources. As the endnotes reveal a total on nearly sixty different documents are cited in *The Devil's Town.*

Acknowledgements

AS NOTED IN THE PRECEDING ESSAY, Ray Hanley's *A Place Apart* is one of my source books. Ray also gave permission to use selected photos from his personal collection. Most helpful of all was his readiness to read the prepublication manuscript to provide corrections and additional context. Similarly, I am indebted to Jim Pfeifer for thoughtfully reading the manuscript. Both Ray and Jim collect Hot Springs gambling memorabilia. Jim also maintains a "History of the Heights" page at Facebook, which is a popular source of historical anecdotes involving Little Rock's 72207 zip code. Finally, about a year ago Jim first informed me of the Club Westwood, which made Las Vegas style gambling available in Little Rock when he and I were high school students in the early 1960s.

Orval Allbritton merits special thanks. Not only has he authored four books about Hot Springs but he also met with me personally and arranged a visit with former FBI Agent Clay White who was the resident FBI Agent in the town from 1954 to 1977. Clay was the "G-man" on the scene when State Police Colonel Lynn Davis shut down Hot Springs gambling in 1967 and also when bombs exploded at The Vapors casino and elsewhere in Hot Springs in 1963.

Lastly I thank Richard DeSpain for sharing reproductions of his numerous paintings and drawings of Hot Springs, spanning many years. The colorful ones of the horse races at Oaklawn Park visually capture a spirit of the town that I have tried to replicate in words.

BIBLIOGRAPHY

HISTORICAL DOCUMENTS

U. S. Senate. *Special Committee to Investigate Organized Crime in Interstate Commerce,* 82nd Congress, First Session, Report Number 275, August 31, 1951, Available: https://goo.gl/tufeFu [Accessed: July 10, 2017]

BOOKS AND COMPILATIONS

Abbott, Shirley, *The Bookmaker's Daughter.* Fayetteville: University of Arkansas Press, 2006

Allbritton, Orval, *Leo and Verne.* Hot Springs, Ark.: Garland County Historical Society, 2003

_______________, *The Mob at The Spa.* Hot Springs, Ark.: Garland County Historical Society, 2011

_______________, *Lawman: The Story of Clay White.* Hot Springs, Ark.: Garland Country Historical Society, 2014

Blumhofer, Edith, *The Assemblies of God: A Popular History.* Springfield, Mo.: Radiant Books, 1985

Brown, Dee, *The American Spa: Hot Springs, Arkansas.* Little Rock, Ark.: Rose Publishing, 1982

Burrough, Bryan, *Public Enemies.* New York: Penguin Group, 2004

Clinton, William J., *My Life: Large Print Edition.* New York: Random House, 2004

Davis, Colonel Lynn, *They Said it Couldn't be Done.* Little Rock, Ark.: Davis Creek Press, 2009

English, T. J., *Havana Nocturne.* New York: William Morrow, 2007

Gosch, Martin and Richard Hammer, *The Last Testament of Lucky Luciano.* New York: Random House, 1981)

Hanley, Ray, *A Place Apart: A Pictorial History of Hot Springs, Arkansas.* Fayetteville, University of Arkansas Press, 2011

Helmer, William and Rick Mattix, *Public Enemies: America's Criminal Past 1919-1940.* New York: Checkmark Books, 1998

Land, Bernard and Myrick, *A Short History of Las Vegas.* Reno: University of Nevada Press, 1999

Lansky, Sandra, *Daughter of the King.* Philadelphia, Pa.: Weinstein Books, 2014

Lester, Jim, *A Man For Arkansas.* Little Rock, Ark.: Rose Publishing, 1976

McMath, Sidney F., *Promises Kept.* Fayetteville: University of Arkansas Press, 2003

Nown, Graham, *Arkansas Godfather.* Little Rock: Butler Center Books, 2011

O'Connor, Sean, "John Ford (1894-1973)," *100 People Who Changed 20th Century America*, ed. Mary Cross. Santa Barbara, Cal.: ABC-CLIO, 2013

Rabb, Selwyn, *Five Families: The Rise, Decline and Resurgence of America's Most Powerful Mafia Empires.* New York: St. Martin's Press, 2006

Reed, Roy, *Faubus: The Life and Times of an American Prodigal.* Fayetteville, Ark.: University of Arkansas Press, 1997

Reppetto, Thomas, *American Mafia: A History of its Rise to Power.* New York: Henry Holt & Co., 2004

Sasuly, Richard, *Bookies and Bettors.* New York: Holt, Reinhart, and Winston, 1982

Schwartz, David, *Cutting the Wire: Gambling Prohibition and the Internet.* Las Vegas: University of Nevada Press, 2005

Sifakis, Carl, *The Mafia Encyclopedia: 3rd Edition.* New York: Checkmark Books, 2005

Scully, Francis, *Hot Springs Arkansas and Hot Spring National Park.* Little Rock, Ark.: Pioneer Press, 1966

Underhill, Robert, *Criminals and Folk Heroes.* New York: Algora Publishing, 2015

Ward, John, *The Arkansas Rockefeller.* Baton Rouge: Louisiana State University Press, 1978

Whitehead, Don, *The FBI Story.* New York: Random House, 1956

ARTICLES

Bachelder, W. K., "The Suppression of Bookie Gambling by a Denial of Telephone and Telegraph Facilities," *Journal of Criminal Law and Criminology* (1949, V. 4, N. 2), 176-77. Available: https://goo.gl/shz2EE [Accessed: July 10, 2017]

Boyle, Robert, "The Hottest Spring in Hot Springs," *Sports Illustrated*, March 19, 1962. Available: http://on.si.com/2tzoHI8 [Accessed: July 7, 2017]

Bright, Beth, "Historian Disappointed by Depiction of Spa City," *Hot Springs Arkansas Sentinel Record*, July 9, 2015. Available: https://goo.gl/CP8xqN [Accessed: July 9, 2017]

Cross, Robert, "Back to Bathhouse Row," *Chicago Tribune*, December 15, 2002. Available: https://goo.gl/oyQK4j [Accessed: July 11, 2017]

Davenport, Walter, "Sin Takes a Hot Bath," *Collier's Weekly*, August 8, 1931

Peck, Lauren, "Abducted in St. Paul!," *Minnesota Good Age*, June 13, 2016. Available: https://goo.gl/4fzcE4 [Accessed: July 8, 2017]

Pierson, James "How Jackie Kennedy Invented the Camelot Legend After JFK's Death," *Daily Beast*, November 12, 2013. Available: http://thebea.st/2sZkMDa [Accessed: July 14, 2017]

Ramsey, Patsy, "A Place at the Table: Hot Spring and the GI Revolt," *Arkansas Historical Quarterly*, V. 59, N. 4 (Winter, 2000)

Seal, Mark, "The Godfather Wars," *Vanity Fair*, February 4, 2009. Available: https://goo.gl/wZhG8E [Accessed: July 9, 2017]

Turner, Wallace, "Hot Springs: Gamblers' Haven," *New York Times*, March 8, 1964. Available: https://goo.gl/dcrZzh [Accessed July 7, 2017]

INTERVIEWS

Abbott, Shirley, "The Bookmaker's Daughter." Interviewed by Host. *PBS Frontline*, May 28, 1996. Available: https://goo.gl/nD83DH [Accessed: July 10, 2017]

Davis, Colonel Lynn "Arkansas State Police Project." Interviewed by Michael Lindsey. *Pryor Center for Arkansas Oral and Visual History: University of Arkansas Libraries*, August 18, 2003

Morris, Roger, "Partners in Power: The Clintons and Their America," Interviewed by Host. *PBS Frontline*, June 13, 1996. Available: https://goo.gl/PwyYQA [Accessed: July 10, 2017]

MASTER'S THESIS

Pierce, James A. "From McMath to Rockefeller: Arkansas Governor and Illegal Gambling in Postwar Hot Springs, 1945 - 1970," *Thesis for Master's Degree* (University of Arkansas, 2008)

MOTION PICTURE

Zanuck, Darryl, *The Man in the Gray Flannel Suit*, Internet Video, directed by Nunnally Johnson (Los Angeles: Twentieth Century Fox, 1956). Available: https://goo.gl/7b3RCW [Accessed: July 11, 2017]

MISCELLANEOUS

Anonymous, "Ma Barker," *The Spell of the West*. Available: https://goo.gl/HL2KfX [Accessed: July 9, 2017]

Anonymous, *Central Distributors*, "About Us." Available: http://bit.ly/2tf2oFO [Accessed: July 12, 2107]

Bellis, Mary, "History of the Water Heater—Invented by Henry Ruud," *ThoughtCo*, August 23, 2016. Available: goo.gl/dcrZzh [Accessed: July 7, 2017]

Federal Reserve Bank of St. Louis and U.S. Bureau of Economic Analysis, "State Per Capita Personal Income." Available: https://goo.gl/FN8Viq [Accessed: July 11, 2017]

Graves, John William, "Poll Tax," *Encyclopedia of Arkansas History and Culture*, July 10, 2012. Available: https://goo.gl/jFgmfy [Accessed: July 8, 2017]

Hendricks, Nancy, "Bill Clinton Boyhood Home," *Encyclopedia of Arkansas History and Culture.* Available: https://goo.gl/WgK8Qp, [July 10, 2017]

Hodge, Michael "The Vapors," *Encyclopedia of Arkansas History and Culture,* February 24, 2014. Available: http://bit.ly/2t4eOF4 [Accessed: July 12, 2017];

Hot Springs (City of), *Airport History.* Available: https://goo.gl/PQdQve [Accessed: July 10, 2017]

May, Allan, "The History of the Race Wire Service," *Race Wire Service,* May 1999. Available: https://goo.gl/3tmbQg [Accessed: July 10, 2017]

Nash, Jay Robert, "Who Was Behind the Kansas City Massacre?" *Annals of Crime.* Available: https://goo.gl/Ndia4G [Accessed: July 9, 2017]

Pfeifer, Jim, "You Bet", *Facebook: History of the Heights.* Available: http://bit.ly/2sQJSUU [Accessed: July 12, 2017]

Richter, Wendy, "Leo Patrick McLaughlin," *The Encyclopedia of Arkansas History and Culture,* October 15, 2008. Available: https://goo.gl/DSGJeR [Accessed: July 8, 2017]

Turzillo, Jane, "Hot Springs Madam Harbored Public Enemy Number 1," *Dark Hearted Women*, September 24, 2012. Available: https://goo.gl/1tksef [Accessed: July 9, 2017]

Williams, C. Fred, "Sid McMath," *The Encyclopedia of Arkansas History and Culture*, April 13, 2016. Available: https://goo.gl/KAzFQi [Accessed: July 11, 2017]

About the Author

PHILIP LEIGH lived in Little Rock until he was twenty-one years old. Thereafter, most of his career was in the investment securities business in Chicago, New York and Florida. Since 2013 he has authored one book annually. *The Devil's Town* is the sixth and the only one about Arkansas. Phil holds a Bachelor of Science in Electrical Engineering from Florida Institute of Technology and a MBA from Northwestern University.

INDEX

SOUTHERN WITHOUT APOLOGY

Free Book Offer

Sign-up for new release notification from SHOTWELL PUBLISHING and receive a FREE DOWNLOADABLE EDITION of *Lies My Teacher Told Me: The True History of the War for Southern Independence* by Dr. Clyde N. Wilson by visiting FreeLiesBook.com or by texting the word "Dixie" to 345-345. You can always unsubscribe and keep the book, so you've got nothing to lose!

Made in the USA
Coppell, TX
26 November 2023